DAN-80   DANTES SUBJECT STANDARDIZED TESTS (DSST)

This is your
PASSBOOK for...

Business Ethics and Society

Test Preparation Study Guide
Questions & Answers

COPYRIGHT NOTICE

This book is SOLELY intended for, is sold ONLY to, and its use is RESTRICTED to individual, bona fide applicants or candidates who qualify by virtue of having seriously filed applications for appropriate license, certificate, professional and/or promotional advancement, higher school matriculation, scholarship, or other legitimate requirements of education and/or governmental authorities.

This book is NOT intended for use, class instruction, tutoring, training, duplication, copying, reprinting, excerption, or adaptation, etc., by:

1) Other publishers
2) Proprietors and/or Instructors of "Coaching" and/or Preparatory Courses
3) Personnel and/or Training Divisions of commercial, industrial, and governmental organizations
4) Schools, colleges, or universities and/or their departments and staffs, including teachers and other personnel
5) Testing Agencies or Bureaus
6) Study groups which seek by the purchase of a single volume to copy and/or duplicate and/or adapt this material for use by the group as a whole without having purchased individual volumes for each of the members of the group
7) Et al.

Such persons would be in violation of appropriate Federal and State statutes.

PROVISION OF LICENSING AGREEMENTS – Recognized educational, commercial, industrial, and governmental institutions and organizations, and others legitimately engaged in educational pursuits, including training, testing, and measurement activities, may address request for a licensing agreement to the copyright owners, who will determine whether, and under what conditions, including fees and charges, the materials in this book may be used them. In other words, a licensing facility exists for the legitimate use of the material in this book on other than an individual basis. However, it is asseverated and affirmed here that the material in this book CANNOT be used without the receipt of the express permission of such a licensing agreement from the Publishers. Inquiries re licensing should be addressed to the company, attention rights and permissions department.

All rights reserved, including the right of reproduction in whole or in part, in any form or by any means, electronic or mechanical, including photocopying, recording, or by any information storage and retrieval system, without permission in writing from the Publisher.

Copyright © 2024 by
National Learning Corporation

212 Michael Drive, Syosset, NY 11791
(516) 921-8888 • www.passbooks.com
E-mail: info@passbooks.com

PUBLISHED IN THE UNITED STATES OF AMERICA

PASSBOOK® SERIES

THE *PASSBOOK® SERIES* has been created to prepare applicants and candidates for the ultimate academic battlefield – the examination room.

At some time in our lives, each and every one of us may be required to take an examination – for validation, matriculation, admission, qualification, registration, certification, or licensure.

Based on the assumption that every applicant or candidate has met the basic formal educational standards, has taken the required number of courses, and read the necessary texts, the *PASSBOOK® SERIES* furnishes the one special preparation which may assure passing with confidence, instead of failing with insecurity. Examination questions – together with answers – are furnished as the basic vehicle for study so that the mysteries of the examination and its compounding difficulties may be eliminated or diminished by a sure method.

This book is meant to help you pass your examination provided that you qualify and are serious in your objective.

The entire field is reviewed through the huge store of content information which is succinctly presented through a provocative and challenging approach – the question-and-answer method.

A climate of success is established by furnishing the correct answers at the end of each test.

You soon learn to recognize types of questions, forms of questions, and patterns of questioning. You may even begin to anticipate expected outcomes.

You perceive that many questions are repeated or adapted so that you can gain acute insights, which may enable you to score many sure points.

You learn how to confront new questions, or types of questions, and to attack them confidently and work out the correct answers.

You note objectives and emphases, and recognize pitfalls and dangers, so that you may make positive educational adjustments.

Moreover, you are kept fully informed in relation to new concepts, methods, practices, and directions in the field.

You discover that you are actually taking the examination all the time: you are preparing for the examination by "taking" an examination, not by reading extraneous and/or supererogatory textbooks.

In short, this PASSBOOK®, used directedly, should be an important factor in helping you to pass your test.

NONTRADITIONAL EDUCATION

Students returning to school as adults bring more varied experience to their studies than do the teenagers who begin college shortly after graduating from high school. As a result, there are numerous programs for students with nontraditional learning curves. Hundreds of colleges and universities grant degrees to people who cannot attend classes at a regular campus or have already learned what the college is supposed to teach.

You can earn nontraditional education credits in many ways:
- Passing standardized exams
- Demonstrating knowledge gained through experience
- Completing campus-based coursework, and
- Taking courses off campus

Some methods of assessing learning for credit are objective, such as standardized tests. Others are more subjective, such as a review of life experiences.

With some help from four hypothetical characters – Alice, Vin, Lynette, and Jorge – this article describes nontraditional ways of earning educational credit. It begins by describing programs in which you can earn a high school diploma without spending 4 years in a classroom. The college picture is more complicated, so it is presented in two parts: one on gaining credit for what you know through course work or experience, and a second on college degree programs. The final section lists resources for locating more information.

Earning High School Credit

People who were prevented from finishing high school as teenagers have several options if they want to do so as adults. Some major cities have back-to-school programs that allow adults to attend high school classes with current students. But the more practical alternatives for most adults are to take the General Educational Development (GED) tests or to earn a high school diploma by demonstrating their skills or taking correspondence classes.

Of course, these options do not match the experience of staying in high school and graduating with one's friends. But they are viable alternatives for adult learners committed to meeting and, often, continuing their educational goals.

GED Program

Alice quit high school her sophomore year and took a job to help support herself, her younger brother, and their newly widowed mother. Now an adult, she wants to earn her high school diploma – and then go on to college. Because her job as head cook and her family responsibilities keep her busy during the day, she plans to get a high school equivalency diploma. She will study for, and take, the GED tests. Every year, about half a million adults earn their high school credentials this way. A GED diploma is accepted in lieu of a high school one by more than 90 percent of employers, colleges, and universities, so it is a good choice for someone like Alice.

The GED testing program is sponsored by the American Council on Education and State and local education departments. It consists of examinations in five subject areas: Writing, science, mathematics, social studies, and literature and the arts. The tests also measure skills such as analytical ability, problem solving, reading comprehension, and ability to understand and apply information. Most of the questions are multiple choice; the writing test includes an essay section on a topic of general interest.

Eligibility rules for taking the exams vary, but some states require that you must be at least 18. Tests are given in English, Spanish, and French. In addition to standard print, versions in large print, Braille, and audiocassette are also available. Total time allotted for the tests is 7 1/2 hours.

The GED tests are not easy. About one-fourth of those who complete the exams every year do not pass. Passing scores are established by administering the tests to a sample of graduating high school seniors. The minimum standard score is set so that about one-third of graduating seniors would not pass the tests if they took them.

Because of the difficulty of the tests, people need to prepare themselves to take them. Often, they start by taking the Official GED Practice Tests, usually available through a local adult education center. Centers are listed in your phone book's blue pages under "Adult Education," "Continuing Education," or "GED." Adult education centers also have information about GED preparation classes and self-study materials. Classes are generally arranged to accommodate adults' work schedules. National Learning Corporation publishes several study guides that aim to thoroughly prepare test-takers for the GED.

School districts, colleges, adult education centers, and community organizations have information about GED testing schedules and practice tests. For more information, contact them, your nearest GED testing center, or:

GED Testing Service
One Dupont Circle, NW, Suite 250
Washington, DC 20036-1163
1(800) 62-MY GED (626-9433)
(202) 939-9490

Skills Demonstration

Adults who have acquired high school level skills through experience might be eligible for the National External Diploma Program. This alternative to the GED does not involve any direct instruction. Instead, adults seeking a high school diploma must demonstrate mastery of 65 competencies in 8 general areas: Communication; computation; occupational preparedness; and self, social, consumer, scientific, and technological awareness.

Mastery is shown through the completion of the tasks. For example, a participant could prove competency in computation by measuring a room for carpeting, figuring out the amount of carpet needed, and computing the cost.

Before being accepted for the program, adults undergo an evaluation. Tests taken at one of the program's offices measure reading, writing, and mathematics abilities. A take-home segment includes a self-assessment of current skills, an individual skill evaluation, and an occupational interest and aptitude test.

Adults accepted for the program have weekly meetings with an assessor. At the meeting, the assessor reviews the participant's work from the previous week. If the task has not been completed properly, the assessor explains the mistake. Participants continue to correct their errors until they master each competency. A high school diploma is awarded upon proven mastery of all 65 competencies.

Fourteen States and the District of Columbia now offer the External Diploma Program. For more information, contact:

    External Diploma Program
    One Dupont Circle, NW, Suite 250
    Washington, DC 20036-1193
    (202) 939-9475

Correspondence and Distance Study

Vin dropped out of high school during his junior year because his family's frequent moves made it difficult for him to continue his studies. He promised himself at the time he dropped out that he would someday finish the courses needed for his diploma. For people like Vin, who prefer to earn a traditional diploma in a nontraditional way, there are about a dozen accredited courses of study for earning a high school diploma by correspondence, or distance study. The programs are either privately run, affiliated with a university, or administered by a State education department.

Distance study diploma programs have no residency requirements, allowing students to continue their studies from almost any location. Depending on the course of study, students need not be enrolled full time and usually have more flexible schedules for finishing their work. Selection of courses ranges from vo-tech to college prep, and some programs place different emphasis on the types of diplomas offered. University affiliated schools, for example, allow qualified students to take college courses along with their high school ones. Students can then apply the college credits toward a degree at that university or transfer them to another institution.

Taking courses by distance study is often more challenging and time consuming than attending classes, especially for adults who have other obligations. Success depends on each student's motivation. Students usually do reading assignments on their own. Written exercises, which they complete and send to an instructor for grading, supplement their reading material.

A list of some accredited high schools that offer diplomas by distance study is available free from the Distance Education and Training Council, formerly known as the National Home Study Council. Request the "DETC Directory of Accredited Institutions" from:

    The Distance Education and Training Council
    1601 18th Street, NW.
    Washington, DC 20009-2529
    (202) 234-5100

Some publications profiling nontraditional college programs include addresses and descriptions of several high school correspondence ones. See the Resources section at the end of this article for more information.

Getting College Credit For What You Know

Adults can receive college credit for prior coursework, by passing examinations, and documenting experiential learning. With help from a college advisor, nontraditional students should assess their skills, establish their educational goals, and determine the number of college credits they might be eligible for.

Even before you meet with a college advisor, you should collect all your school and training records. Then, make a list of all knowledge and abilities acquired through experience, no matter how irrelevant they seem to your chosen field. Next, determine your educational goals: What specific field do you wish to study? What kind of a degree do you want? Finally, determine how your past work fits into the field of study. Later on, you will evaluate educational programs to find one that's right for you.

People who have complex educational or experiential learning histories might want to have their learning evaluated by the Regents Credit Bank. The Credit Bank, operated by Regents College of the University of the State of New York, allows people to consolidate credits earned through college, experience, or other methods. Special assessments are available for Regents College enrollees whose knowledge in a specific field cannot be adequately evaluated by standardized exams. For more information, contact the Regents Credit Bank at:

Regents College
7 Columbia Circle
Albany, NY 12203-5159
(518) 464-8500

Credit For Prior College Coursework

When Lynette was in college during the 1970s, she attended several different schools and took a variety of courses. She did well in some classes and poorly in others. Now that she is a successful business owner and has more focus, Lynette thinks she should forget about her previous coursework and start from scratch. Instead, she should start from where she is.

Lynette should have all her transcripts sent to the colleges or universities of her choice and let an admissions officer determine which classes are applicable toward a degree. A few credits here and there may not seem like much, but they add up. Even if the subjects do not seem relevant to any major, they might be counted as elective credits toward a degree. And comparing the cost of transcripts with the cost of college courses, it makes sense to spend a few dollars per transcript for a chance to save hundreds, and perhaps thousands, of dollars in books and tuition.

Rules for transferring credits apply to all prior coursework at accredited colleges and universities, whether done on campus or off. Courses completed off campus, often called extended learning, include those available to students through independent study and correspondence. Many schools have extended learning programs; Brigham Young University, for example, offers more than 300 courses through its Department of Independent Study. One type of extended learning is distance learning, a form of correspondence study by technological means such as television, video and audio, CD-ROM, electronic mail, and computer tutorials. See the Resources section at the end of this article for more information about publications available from the National University Continuing Education Association.

Any previously earned college credits should be considered for transfer, no matter what the subject or the grade received. Many schools do not accept the transfer of courses graded below a C or ones taken more than a designated number of years ago. Some colleges and universities also have limits on the number of credits that can be transferred and applied toward a degree. But not all do. For example, Thomas Edison State College, New Jersey's State college for adults, accepts the transfer of all 120 hours of credit required for a baccalaureate degree – provided all the credits are transferred from regionally accredited schools, no more than 80 are at the junior college level, and the student's grades overall and in the field of study average out to C.

To assign credit for prior coursework, most schools require original transcripts. This means you must complete a form or send a written, signed request to have your transcripts released directly to a college or university. Once you have chosen the schools you want to apply to, contact the schools you attended before. Find out how much each transcript costs, and ask them to send your transcripts to the ones you are applying to. Write a letter that includes your name (and names used during attendance, if different) and dates of attendance, along with the names and addresses of the schools to which your transcripts should be sent. Include payment and mail to the registrar at the schools you have attended. The registrar's office will process your request and send an official transcript of your coursework to the colleges or universities you have designated.

Credit For Noncollege Courses

Colleges and universities are not the only ones that offer classes. Volunteer organizations and employers often provide formal training worth college credit. The American Council on Education has two programs that assess thousands of specific courses and make recommendations on the amount of college credit they are worth. Colleges and universities accept the recommendations or use them as guidelines.

One program evaluates educational courses sponsored by government agencies, business and industry, labor unions, and professional and voluntary organizations. It is the Program on Noncollegiate Sponsored Instruction (PONSI). Some of the training seminars Alice has participated in covered topics such as food preparation, kitchen safety, and nutrition. Although she has not yet earned her GED, Alice can earn college credit because of her completion of these formal job-training seminars. The number of credits each seminar is worth does not hinge on Alice's current eligibility for college enrollment.

The other program evaluates courses offered by the Army, Navy, Air Force, Marines, Coast Guard, and Department of Defense. It is the Military Evaluations Program. Jorge has never attended college, but the engineering technology classes he completed as part of his military training are worth college credit. And as an Army veteran, Jorge is eligible for a service that takes the evaluations one step further. The Army/American Council on Education Registry Transcript System (AARTS) will provide Jorge with an individualized transcript of American Council on Education credit recommendations for all courses he completed, the military occupational specialties (MOS's) he held, and examinations he passed while in the Army. All Army and National Guard enlisted personnel and veterans who enlisted after October 1981 are eligible for the transcript. Similar services are being considered by the Navy and Marine Corps.

To obtain a free transcript, see your Army Education Center for a 5454R transcript request form. Include your name, Social Security number, basic active service date, and complete address where you want the transcript sent. Mail your request to:
AARTS Operations Center
415 McPherson Ave.
Fort Leavenworth, KS 66027-1373

Recommendations for PONSI are published in *The National Guide to Educational Credit for Training Programs;* military program recommendations are in *The Guide to the Evaluation of Educational Experiences in the Armed Forces.* See the Resources section at the end of this article for more information about these publications.

Former military personnel who took a foreign language course through the Defense Language Institute may request course transcripts by sending their name, Social Security number, course title, duration of the course, and graduation date to:

    Commandant, Defense Language Institute
    Attn: ATFL-DAA-AR
    Transcripts
    Presidio of Monterey
    Monterey, CA 93944-5006

Not all of Jorge's and Alice's courses have been assessed by the American Council on Education. Training courses that have no Council credit recommendation should still be assessed by an advisor at the schools they want to attend. Course descriptions, class notes, test scores, and other documentation may be helpful for comparing training courses to their college equivalents. An oral examination or other demonstration of competency might also be required.

There is no guarantee you will receive all the credits you are seeking – but you certainly won't if you make no attempt.

Credit By Examination

Standardized tests are the best-known method of receiving college credit without taking courses. These exams are often taken by high school students seeking advanced placement for college, but they are also available to adult learners. Testing programs and colleges and universities offer exams in a number of subjects. Two U.S. Government institutes have foreign language exams for employees that also may be worth college credit.

It is important to understand that receiving a passing score on these exams does not mean you get college credit automatically. Each school determines which test results it will accept, minimum scores required, how scores are converted for credit, and the amount of credit, if any, to be assigned. Most colleges and universities accept the American Council on Education credit recommendations, published every other year in the 250-page *Guide to Educational Credit by Examination*. For more information, contact:

    The American Council on Education
    Credit by Examination Program
    One Dupont Circle, Suite 250
    Washington, DC 20036-1193
    (202) 939-9434

Testing programs:

You might know some of the five national testing programs by their acronyms or initials: CLEP, ACT PEP: RCE, DANTES, AP, and NOCTI. (The meanings of these initialisms are explained below.) There is some overlap among programs; for example, four of them have introductory accounting exams. Since you will not be awarded credit more than once for a specific subject, you should carefully evaluate each program for the subject exams you wish to take. And before taking an exam, make sure you will be awarded credit by the college or university you plan to attend.

CLEP (College-Level Examination Program), administered by the College Board, is the most widely accepted of the national testing programs; more than 2,800 accredited schools award credit for passing exam scores. Each test covers material taught in basic

undergraduate courses. There are five general exams – English composition, humanities, college mathematics, natural sciences, and social sciences and history – and many subject exams. Most exams are entirely multiple-choice, but English composition exams may include an essay section. For more information, contact:
    CLEP
    P.O. Box 6600
    Princeton, NJ 08541-6600
    (609) 771-7865

ACT PEP: RCE (American College Testing Proficiency Exam Program: Regents College Examinations) tests are given in 38 subjects within arts and sciences, business, education, and nursing. Each exam is recommended for either lower- or upper-level credit. Exams contain either objective or extended response questions, and are graded according to a standard score, letter grade, or pass/fail. Fees vary, depending on the subject and type of exam. For more information or to request free study guides, contact:
    ACT PEP: Regents College Examinations
    P.O. Box 4014
    Iowa City, IA 52243
    (319) 337-1387
    (New York State residents must contact Regents College directly.)

DANTES (Defense Activity for Nontraditional Education Support) standardized tests are developed by the Educational Testing Service for the Department of Defense. Originally administered only to military personnel, the exams have been available to the public since 1983. About 50 subject tests cover business, mathematics, social science, physical science, humanities, foreign languages, and applied technology. Most of the tests consist entirely of multiple-choice questions. Schools determine their own administering fees and testing schedules. For more information or to request free study sheets, contact:
    DANTES Program Office
    Mail Stop 31-X
    Educational Testing Service
    Princeton, NJ 08541
    1(800) 257-9484

The AP (Advanced Placement) Program is a cooperative effort between secondary schools and colleges and universities. AP exams are developed each year by committees of college and high school faculty appointed by the College Board and assisted by consultants from the Educational Testing Service. Subjects include arts and languages, natural sciences, computer science, social sciences, history, and mathematics. Most tests are 2 or 3 hours long and include both multiple-choice and essay questions. AP courses are available to help students prepare for exams, which are offered in the spring. For more information about the Advanced Placement Program, contact:
    Advanced Placement Services
    P.O. Box 6671
    Princeton, NJ 08541-6671
    (609) 771-7300

NOCTI (National Occupational Competency Testing Institute) assessments are designed for people like Alice, who have vocational-technical skills that cannot be evaluated by other tests. NOCTI assesses competency at two levels: Student/job ready and teacher/experienced worker. Standardized evaluations are available for occupations such as auto-body repair, electronics, mechanical drafting, quantity food preparation, and upholstering. The tests consist of multiple-choice questions and a performance component. Other services include workshops, customized assessments, and pre-testing. For more information, contact:

NOCTI
500 N. Bronson Ave.
Ferris State University
Big Rapids, MI 49307
(616) 796-4699

Colleges and universities:

Many colleges and universities have credit-by-exam programs, through which students earn credit by passing a comprehensive exam for a course offered by the institution. Among the most widely recognized are the programs at Ohio University, the University of North Carolina, Thomas Edison State College, and New York University.

Ohio University offers about 150 examinations for credit. In addition, you may sometimes arrange to take special examinations in non-laboratory courses offered at Ohio University. To take a test for credit, you must enroll in the course. If you plan to transfer the credit earned, you also need written permission from an official at your school. Books and study materials are available, for a cost, through the university. Exams must be taken within 6 months of the enrollment date; most last 3 hours. You may arrange to take the exam off campus if you do not live near the university.

Ohio University is on the quarter-hour system; most courses are worth 4 quarter hours, the equivalent of 3 semester hours. For more information, contact:

Independent Study
Tupper Hall 302
Ohio University
Athens, OH 45701-2979
1(800) 444-2910
(614) 593-2910

The University of North Carolina offers a credit-by-examination option for 140 independent study (correspondence) courses in foreign languages, humanities, social sciences, mathematics, business administration, education, electrical and computer engineering, health administration, and natural sciences. To take an exam, you must request and receive approval from both the course instructor and the independent studies department. Exams must be taken within six months of enrollment, and you may register for no more than two at a time. If you are not near the University's Chapel Hill campus, you may take your exam under supervision at an accredited college, university, community college, or technical institute. For more information, contact:

Independent Studies
CB #1020, The Friday Center
UNC-Chapel Hill
Chapel Hill, NC 27599-1020
1(800) 862-5669 / (919) 962-1134

The Thomas Edison College Examination Program offers more than 50 exams in liberal arts, business, and professional areas. Thomas Edison State College administers tests twice a month in Trenton, New Jersey; however, students may arrange to take their tests with a proctor at any accredited American college or university or U.S. military base. Most of the tests are multiple choice; some also include short answer or essay questions. Time limits range from 90 minutes to 4 hours, depending on the exam. For more information, contact:

>Thomas Edison State College
>TECEP, Office of Testing and Assessment
>101 W. State Street
>Trenton, NJ 08608-1176
>(609) 633-2844

New York University's Foreign Language Program offers proficiency exams in more than 40 languages, from Albanian to Yiddish. Two exams are available in each language: The 12-point test is equivalent to 4 undergraduate semesters, and the 16-point exam may lead to upper level credit. The tests are given at the university's Foreign Language Department throughout the year.

Proof of foreign language proficiency does not guarantee college credit. Some colleges and universities accept transcripts only for languages commonly taught, such as French and Spanish. Nontraditional programs are more likely than traditional ones to grant credit for proficiency in other languages.

For an informational brochure and registration form for NYU's foreign language proficiency exams, contact:

>New York University
>Foreign Language Department
>48 Cooper Square, Room 107
>New York, NY 10003
>(212) 998-7030

Government institutes:

The Defense Language Institute and Foreign Service Institute administer foreign language proficiency exams for personnel stationed abroad. Usually, the tests are given at the end of intensive language courses or upon completion of service overseas. But some people – like Jorge, who knows Spanish – speak another language fluently and may be allowed to take a proficiency exam in that language before completing their tour of duty. Contact one of the offices listed below to obtain transcripts of those scores. Proof of proficiency does not guarantee college credit, however, as discussed above.

To request score reports from the Defense Language Institute for Defense Language Proficiency Tests, send your name, Social Security number, language for which you were tested, and, most importantly, when and where you took the exam to:

>Commandant, Defense Language Institute
>Attn: ATFL-ES-T
>DLPT Score Report Request
>Presidio of Monterey
>Monterey, CA 93944-5006

To request transcripts of scores for Foreign Service Institute exams, send your name, Social Security number, language for which you were tested, and dates or year of exams to:

Foreign Service Institute
Arlington Hall
4020 Arlington Boulevard
Rosslyn, VA 22204-1500
Attn: Testing Office (Send your request to the attention of the testing office of the foreign language in which you were tested)

Credit For Experience

Experiential learning credit may be given for knowledge gained through job responsibilities, personal hobbies, volunteer opportunities, homemaking, and other experiences. Colleges and universities base credit awards on the knowledge you have attained, not for the experience alone. In addition, the knowledge must be college level; not just any learning will do. Throwing horseshoes as a hobby is not likely to be worth college credit. But if you've done research on how and where the sport originated, visited blacksmiths, organized tournaments, and written a column for a trade journal — well, that's a horseshoe of a different color.

Adults attempting to get credit for their experience should be forewarned: Having your experience evaluated for college credit is time-consuming, tedious work — not an easy shortcut for people who want quick-fix college credits. And not all experience, no matter how valuable, is the equivalent of college courses.

Requesting college credit for your experiential learning can be tricky. You should get assistance from a credit evaluations officer at the school you plan to attend, but you should also have a general idea of what your knowledge is worth. A common method for converting knowledge into credit is to use a college catalog. Find course titles and descriptions that match what you have learned through experience, and request the number of credits offered for those courses.

Once you know what credit to ask for, you must usually present your case in writing to officials at the college you plan to attend. The most common form of presenting experiential learning for credit is the portfolio. A portfolio is a written record of your knowledge along with a request for equivalent college credit. It includes an identification and description of the knowledge for which you are requesting credit, an explanatory essay of how the knowledge was gained and how it fits into your educational plans, documentation that you have acquired such knowledge, and a request for college credit. Required elements of a portfolio vary by schools but generally follow those guidelines.

In identifying knowledge you have gained, be specific about exactly what you have learned. For example, it is not enough for Lynette to say she runs a business. She must identify the knowledge she has gained from running it, such as personnel management, tax law, marketing strategy, and inventory review. She must also include brief descriptions about her knowledge of each to support her claims of having those skills.

The essay gives you a chance to relay something about who you are. It should address your educational goals, include relevant autobiographical details, and be well organized, neat, and convey confidence. In his essay, Jorge might first state his goal of becoming an engineer. Then he would explain why he joined the Army, where he got hands-on training and experience in developing and servicing electronic equipment.

This, he would say, led to his hobby of creating remote-controlled model cars, of which he has built 20. His conclusion would highlight his accomplishments and tie them to his desire to become an electronic engineer.

Documentation is evidence that you've learned what you claim to have learned. You can show proof of knowledge in a variety of ways, including audio or video recordings, letters from current or former employers describing your specific duties and job performance, blueprints, photographs or artwork, and transcripts of certifying exams for professional licenses and certification – such as Alice's certification from the American Culinary Federation. Although documentation can take many forms, written proof alone is not always enough. If it is impossible to document your knowledge in writing, find out if your experiential learning can be assessed through supplemental oral exams by a faculty expert.

Earning a College Degree

Nontraditional students often have work, family, and financial obligations that prevent them from quitting their jobs to attend school full time. Can they still meet their educational goals? Yes.

More than 150 accredited colleges and universities have nontraditional bachelor's degree programs that require students to spend little or no time on campus; over 300 others have nontraditional campus-based degree programs. Some of those schools, as well as most junior and community colleges, offer associate's degrees nontraditionally. Each school with a nontraditional course of study determines its own rules for awarding credit for prior coursework, exams, or experience, as discussed previously. Most have charges on top of tuition for providing these special services.

Several publications profile nontraditional degree programs; see the Resources section at the end of this article for more information. To determine which school best fits your academic profile and educational goals, first list your criteria. Then, evaluate nontraditional programs based on their accreditation, features, residency requirements, and expenses. Once you have chosen several schools to explore further, write to them for more information. Detailed explanations of school policies should help you decide which ones you want to apply to.

Get beyond the printed word – especially the glowing words each school writes about itself. Check out the schools you are considering with higher education authorities, alumni, employers, family members, and friends. If possible, visit the campus to talk to students and instructors and sit in on a few classes, even if you will be completing most or all of your work off campus. Ask school officials questions about such things as enrollment numbers, graduation rate, faculty qualifications, and confusing details about the application process or academic policies. After you have thoroughly investigated each prospective college or university, you can make an informed decision about which is right for you.

Accreditation

Accreditation is a process colleges and universities submit to voluntarily for getting their credentials. An accredited school has been investigated and visited by teams of observers and has periodic inspections by a private accrediting agency. The initial review can take two years or more.

Regional agencies accredit entire schools, and professional agencies accredit either specialized schools or departments within schools. Although there are no national accrediting standards, not just any accreditation will do. Countless "accreditation associations" have been invented by schools, many of which have no academic programs and sell phony degrees, to accredit themselves. But 6 regional and about 80 professional accrediting associations in the United States are recognized by the U.S. Department of Education or the Commission on Recognition of Postsecondary Accreditation. When checking accreditation, these are the names to look for. For more information about accreditation and accrediting agencies, contact:

> Institutional Participation Oversight Service Accreditation and State Liaison Division
> U.S. Department of Education
> ROB 3, Room 3915
> 600 Independence Ave., SW
> Washington, DC 20202-5244
> (202) 708-7417

Because accreditation is not mandatory, lack of accreditation does not necessarily mean a school or program is bad. Some schools choose not to apply for accreditation, are in the process of applying, or have educational methods too unconventional for an accrediting association's standards. For the nontraditional student, however, earning a degree from a college or university with recognized accreditation is an especially important consideration. Although nontraditional education is becoming more widely accepted, it is not yet mainstream. Employers skeptical of a degree earned in a nontraditional manner are likely to be even less accepting of one from an unaccredited school.

Program Features

Because nontraditional students have diverse educational objectives, nontraditional schools are diverse in what they offer. Some programs are geared toward helping students organize their scattered educational credits to get a degree as quickly as possible. Others cater to those who may have specific credits or experience but need assistance in completing requirements. Whatever your educational profile, you should look for a program that works with you in obtaining your educational goals.

A few nontraditional programs have special admissions policies for adult learners like Alice, who plan to earn their GEDs but want to enroll in college in the meantime. Other features of nontraditional programs include individualized learning agreements, intensive academic counseling, cooperative learning and internship placement, and waiver of some prerequisites or other requirements – as well as college credit for prior coursework, examinations, and experiential learning, all discussed previously.

Lynette, whose primary goal is to finish her degree, wants to earn maximum credits for her business experience. She will look for programs that do not limit the number of credits awarded for equivalency exams and experiential learning. And since well-documented proof of knowledge is essential for earning experiential learning credits, Lynette should make sure the program she chooses provides assistance to students submitting a portfolio.

Jorge, on the other hand, has more credits than he needs in certain areas and is willing to forego some. To become an engineer, he must have a bachelor's degree; but because he is accustomed to hands-on learning, Jorge is interested in getting experience as he gains more technical skills. He will concentrate on finding schools with strong cooperative education, supervised fieldwork, or internship programs.

Residency Requirements

Programs are sometimes deemed nontraditional because of their residency requirements. Many people think of residency for colleges and universities in terms of tuition, with in-state students paying less than out-of-state ones. Residency also may refer to where a student lives, either on or off campus, while attending school.

But in nontraditional education, residency usually refers to how much time students must spend on campus, regardless of whether they attend classes there. In some nontraditional programs, students need not ever step foot on campus. Others require only a very short residency, such as one day or a few weeks. Many schools have standard residency requirements of several semesters but schedule classes for evenings or weekends to accommodate working adults.

Lynette, who previously took courses by independent study, prefers to earn credits by distance study. She will focus on schools that have no residency requirement. Several colleges and universities have nonresident degree completion programs for adults with some college credit. Under the direction of a faculty advisor, students devise a plan for earning their remaining credits. Methods for earning credits include independent study, distance learning, seminars, supervised fieldwork, and group study at arranged sites. Students may have to earn a certain number of credits through the degree-granting institution. But many programs allow students to take courses at accredited schools of their choice for transfer toward their degree.

Alice wants to attend lectures but has an unpredictable schedule. Her best course of action will be to seek out short residency programs that require students to attend seminars once or twice a semester. She can take courses that are televised and videotape them to watch when her schedule permits, with the seminars helping to ensure that she properly completes her coursework. Many colleges and universities with short residency requirements also permit students to earn some credits elsewhere, by whatever means the student chooses.

Some fields of study require classroom instruction. As Jorge will discover, few colleges and universities allow students to earn a bachelor's degree in engineering entirely through independent study. Nontraditional residency programs are designed to accommodate adults' daytime work schedules. Jorge should look for programs offering evening, weekend, summer, and accelerated courses.

Tuition and Other Expenses

The final decisions about which schools Alice, Jorge, and Lynette attend may hinge in large part on a single issue: Cost. And rising tuition is only part of the equation. Beginning with application fees and continuing through graduation fees, college expenses add up.

Traditional and nontraditional students have some expenses in common, such as the cost of books and other materials. Tuition might even be the same for some courses, especially for colleges and universities offering standard ones at unusual times. But for nontraditional programs, students may also pay fees for services such as credit or transcript review, evaluation, advisement, and portfolio assessment.

Students are also responsible for postage and handling or setup expenses for independent study courses, as well as for all examination and transcript fees for transferring credits. Usually, the more nontraditional the program, the more detailed the fees. Some schools charge a yearly enrollment fee rather than tuition for degree completion candidates who want their files to remain active.

Although tuition and fees might seem expensive, most educators tell you not to let money come between you and your educational goals. Talk to someone in the financial aid department of the school you plan to attend or check your library for publications about financial aid sources. The U.S. Department of Education publishes a guide to Federal aid programs such as Pell Grants, student loans, and work-study. To order the free 74-page booklet, *The Student Guide: Financial Aid from the U.S. Department of Education,* contact:

Federal Student Aid Information Center
P.O. Box 84
Washington, DC 20044
1 (800) 4FED-AID (433-3243)

Resources

Information on how to earn a high school diploma or college degree without following the usual routes is available from several organizations and in numerous publications. Information on nontraditional graduate degree programs, available for master's through doctoral level, though not discussed in this article, can usually be obtained from the same resources that detail bachelor's degree programs.

National Learning Corporation publishes study guides for all of these exams, for both general examinations and tests in specific subject areas. To order study guides, or to browse their catalog featuring more than 5,000 titles, visit NLC online at www.passbooks.com, or contact them by phone at (800) 632-8888.

Organizations

Adult learners should always contact their local school system, community college, or university to learn about programs that are readily available. The following national organizations can also supply information:

American Council on Education
One Dupont Circle
Washington, DC 20036-1193
(202) 939-9300

Within the American Council on Education, the Center for Adult Learning and Educational Credentials administers the National External Diploma Program, the GED Program, the Program on Noncollegiate Sponsored Instruction, the Credit by Examination Program, and the Military Evaluations Program.

DANTES Subject Standardized Tests

INTRODUCTION

The DANTES (Defense Activity for Non-Traditional Education Support) subject standardized tests are comprehensive college and graduate level examinations given by the Armed Forces, colleges and graduate schools as end-of-subject course evaluation final examinations or to obtain college equivalency credits in the various subject areas tested.

The DANTES Examination Program enables students to obtain college credit for what they have learned on the job, through self-study, personal interest, correspondence courses or by any other means. It is used by colleges and universities to award college credit to students who demonstrate that they know as much as students completing an equivalent college course. It is a cost-efficient, time-saving way for students to use their knowledge to accomplish their educational goals.

Most schools accept the American Council on Education (ACE) recommendations for the minimum score required and the amount of credit awarded, but not all schools do. Be sure to check the policy regarding the score level required for credit and the number of credits to be awarded.

Not all tests are accepted by all institutions. Even when a test is accepted by an institution, it may not be acceptable for every program at that institution. Before considering testing, ascertain the acceptability of a specific test for a particular course.

Colleges and universities that administer DANTES tests may administer them to any applicant – or they may administer the tests only to students registered at their institution. Decisions about who will be allowed to test are made by the school. Students should contact the test center to determine current policies and schedules for DANTES testing.

Colleges and universities authorized to administer DANTES tests usually do so throughout the calendar year. Each school sets its own fee for test administration and establishes its own testing schedule. Contact the representative at the administering school directly to make arrangements for testing.

Checklist
For Students

✓ Visit **www.getcollegecredit.com** to obtain a list of tests, fact sheets, test preparation materials, participating colleges and universities, and much more.

✓ Contact your school advisor to confirm that the DSST you selected will fit into your curriculum.

✓ Consult the ***DSST Candidate Information Bulletin*** for answers to specific questions.

✓ Contact the test site to schedule your test.

✓ Prepare for your examination by using the fact sheet as a guide.

✓ Take the test.

If you would like a score report sent to your college or university, it is a good idea to bring the four-digit code with you. You must write the DSST Test Center Code for that institution on your answer sheet at the time of testing. DSST Test Center Codes are noted in the DSST Participating Colleges and Universities listing on the Web site.

If you prefer to send a score report to an institution at a later date, there is a transcript fee of $20 for each transcript ordered.

Thomson Prometric
DSST Program
2000 Lenox Drive, Third Floor
Lawrenceville, NJ 08648

Toll-free: 877-471-9860
609-895-5011

E-mail: pnj-dsst@thomson.com

MAKING A COLLEGE DEGREE WITHIN YOUR REACH

Today, there are many educational alternatives to the classroom—you can learn from your job, your reading, your independent study, and special interests you pursue. You may already have learned the subject matter covered by some college-level courses.

The DSST Program is a nationally recognized testing program that gives you the opportunity to receive college credit for learning acquired outside the traditional college classroom. Colleges and universities throughout the United States administer the program, developed by Thomson Prometric, year-round. Annually, over 90,000 DSSTs are administered to individuals who are interested in continuing their education. Take advantage of the DSST testing program; it speeds the educational process and provides the flexibility adults need, making earning a degree more feasible.

Since requirements differ from college to college, please check with the credit-awarding institution before taking a DSST. More than 1,800 colleges and universities currently award credit for DSSTs, and the number is growing every day. You can choose from 37 test titles in the areas of Social Science, Business, Mathematics, Applied Technology, Humanities, and Physical Science. A brief description of each examination is found on the pages that follow.

Reach Your Career Goals Through DSSTs

Use DSSTs to help you earn your degree, get a promotion, or simply demonstrate that you have college-level knowledge in subjects relevant to your work.

Save Time...

You don't have to sit through classes when you have previously acquired the knowledge or experience for most of what is being taught and can learn the rest yourself. You might be able to bypass introductory-level courses in subject areas you already know.

Save Money...

DSSTs save you money because the classes you bypass by earning credit through the DSST Program are classes you won't have to pay for on your way to earning your degree. You can use the money instead to take more advanced courses that can be more challenging and rewarding.

Improve Your Chances for Admission to College

Each college has its own admission policies; however, having passing scores for DSSTs on your transcript can provide strong evidence of how well you can perform at the college level.

Gain Confidence Performing at a College Level

Many adults returning to college find that lack of confidence is often the greatest hurdle to overcome. Passing a DSST demonstrates your ability to perform on a college level.

Make Up for Courses You May Have Missed
You may be ready to graduate from college and find that you are a few credits short of earning your degree. By using semester breaks, vacation time, or leisure time to study independently, you can prepare to take one or more DSSTs, fulfill your academic requirements, and graduate on time.

If You Cannot Attend Regularly Scheduled Classes...
If your lifestyle or responsibilities prevent you from attending regularly scheduled classes, you can earn your college degree from a college offering an external degree program. The DSST Program allows you to earn your degree by study and experience outside the traditional classroom.

Many colleges and universities offer external degree or distance learning programs. For additional information, contact the college you plan to attend or:

Center for Lifelong Learning
American Council on Education
One DuPont Circle NW, Suite 250
Washington, DC 20036
202-939-9475
www.acenet.edu
(Select "Center for Lifelong Learning" under "Programs & Services"
for more information)

Fact Sheets
For each test, there is a Fact Sheet that outlines the topics covered by each test and includes a list of sample questions, a list of recommended references of books that would be useful for review, and the number of credits awarded for a passing score as recommended by the American Council on Education (ACE). *Please note that some schools require scores that are higher than the minimum ACE-recommended passing score.* It is suggested that you check with your college or university to determine what score they require in order to earn credit. You can obtain Fact Sheets by:
- Downloading them from www.getcollegecredit.com
- E-mailing a request to pnj-dsst@thomson.com
- Completing a Candidate Publications Order Form

DSST Online Practice Tests
DSST online practice tests contain items that reflect a *partial range of difficulty* identified in the Content Outline section on each Fact Sheet. There is an online DSST Practice Test in the following categories:
- Mathematics
- Social Science
- Business
- Physical Science
- Applied Technology
- Humanities

Although the online DSST Practice Test questions do not indicate the full range of difficulty you would find in an actual DSST test, they will help you assess your knowledge level. Each online DSST Practice Test can be purchased by visiting www.getcollegecredit.com and clicking on DSST Practice Exams.

TAKING DSST EXAMINATIONS

Earning College Credit for DSST Examinations

To find out if the college of your choice awards credit for passing DSST scores, contact the admissions office or counseling and testing office. The college can also provide information on the scores required for awarding credit, the number of credit hours awarded, and any courses that can be bypassed with satisfactory scores.

It is important that you contact the institution of your choice as early as possible since credit-awarding policies differ among colleges and universities.

Where to Take DSSTs

DSSTs are administered at colleges and universities nationwide. Each location determines the frequency and scheduling of test administrations. To obtain the most current list of participating DSST colleges and universities:
- Visit and download the information from www.getcollegecredit.com
- E-mail pnj-dsst@thomson.com

Scheduling Your Examination

Please be aware that some colleges and universities provide DSST testing services to enrolled students only. After you have selected a college or university that administers DSSTs, you will need to contact them to schedule your test date.

The fee to take a DSST is $60 per test. This fee entitles you to two score reports after the test is scored. One will be sent directly to you and the other will be sent to the college or university that you designate on your answer sheet. You may pay the test fee with a certified check or U.S. money order made payable to Thomson Prometric or you may charge the test fee to your Visa, MasterCard or American Express credit card. Note: The credit card statement will reflect a charge from Thomson Prometric for all DSST examinations. *(Declined credit card charges will be assessed an additional $25 processing fee.)*

In addition, the test site may also require a test administration fee for each examination, to be paid directly to the institution. Contact the test site to determine its administration fee and payment policy.

Other Testing Arrangements

If you are unable to find a participating DSST college or university in your area, you may want to contact the testing office of a local accredited college or university to determine whether a representative from that office will agree to administer the test(s) for you.

The school's representative should then contact the DSST Program at 866-794-3497 to arrange for this administration. If you are unable to locate a test site, contact Thomson Prometric for assistance at pnj-dsst@thomson.com or 866-794-3497.

Testing Accommodations for Students with Disabilities

Thomson Prometric is committed to serving test takers with disabilities by providing services and reasonable testing accommodations as set forth in the provisions of the *Americans with Disabilities Act* (ADA). If you have a disability, as prescribed by the ADA, and require special testing services or arrangements, please contact the test administrator at the test site. You will be asked to submit to the test administrator documentation of your disability and your request for special accommodations. The test administrator will then forward your documentation along with your request for testing accommodations to Thomson Prometric for approval.

Please submit your request as far in advance of your test date as possible so that the necessary accommodations can be made. Only test takers with documented disabilities are eligible for special accommodations.

On the Day of the Examination

It is important to review this information and to have the correct identification present on the day of the examination:

- Arrive on time as a courtesy to the test administrator.
- Bring a valid form of government-issued identification that includes a current photo and your signature (acceptable documents include a driver's license, passport, state-issued identification card or military identification). *Anyone who fails to present valid identification will not be allowed to test.*
- Bring several No. 2 (soft-lead) sharpened pencils with good erasers, a watch, and a black pen if you will be writing an essay.
- Do not bring books or papers.
- Do not bring an alarm watch that beeps, a telephone, or a phone beeper into the testing room.
- The use of nonprogrammable calculators, slide rules, scratch paper and/or other materials is permitted for some of the tests.

DSST SCORING POLICIES

Your DSST examination scores are reported only to you, unless you request that they be sent elsewhere. If you want your scores sent to your college, you must provide the correct DSST code number of the school on your answer sheet at the time you take the test. See the *DSST Directory of Colleges and Universities* on the Web site www.getcollegecredit.com.

If your institution is not listed, contact Thomson Prometric at 866-794-3497 to establish a code number. (Some schools may require a student to be enrolled prior to receiving a score report.)

Receiving Your Score Report

Allow approximately four weeks after testing to receive your score report.

Calling DSST Customer Service before the required four-week score processing time has elapsed will not expedite the processing of your scores. Due to privacy and security requirements, scores will not be reported to students over the telephone under any circumstance.

Scoring of Principles of Public Speaking Speeches

The speech portion of the *Principles of Public Speaking* examination will be sent to speech raters who are faculty members at accredited colleges that currently teach or have previously taught the course. Scores for the *Principles of Public Speaking* examination are available six to eight weeks from receipt by Thomson Prometric. If you take the *Principles of Public Speaking* examination and fail (either the objective, speech portion, or both), you must follow the retesting policy waiting period of six months (180 days) before retaking the entire exam.

Essays
    The essays for *Ethics in America* and *Technical Writing* are <u>optional</u> and thus are not scored by raters. The essays are forwarded to the college or university that you designate, along with your score report, for their use in determining the award of credit. <u>Before taking the *Ethics in America* or *Technical Writing* examinations, check with your college or university to determine whether the essay is required.</u>
    NOTE: *Principles of Public Speaking* speech topic cassette tapes and essays are kept on file at Thomson Prometric for one year from the date of administration.

How to Get Transcripts
    There is a $20 fee for each transcript you request. Payment must be in the form of a certified check, U.S. money order payable to Thomson Prometric, or credit card. Personal checks and debit cards are NOT an acceptable method of payment. One transcript may include scores for one or more examinations taken. To request a transcript, download the Transcript Order Form from www.getcollegecredit.com.

DESCRIPTION OF THE DSST EXAMINATIONS

Mathematics
• **Fundamentals of College Algebra** covers mathematical concepts such as fundamental algebraic operations; linear, absolute value; quadratic equations, inequalities, radials, exponents and logarithms, factoring polynomials and graphing. The use of a nonprogrammable, handheld calculator is permitted.

• **Principles of Statistics** tests the understanding of the various topics of statistics, both qualitatively and quantitatively, and the ability to apply statistical methods to solve a variety of problems. The topics included in this test are descriptive statistics; correlation and regression; probability; chance models and sampling and tests of significance. The use of a nonprogrammable, handheld calculator is permitted.

Social Science
• **Art of the Western World** deals with the history of art during the following periods: classical; Romanesque and Gothic; early Renaissance; high Renaissance, Baroque; rococo; neoclassicism and romanticism; realism, impressionism and post-impressionism; early twentieth century; and post-World War II.

• **Western Europe Since 1945** tests the knowledge of basic facts and terms and the understanding of concepts and principles related to the areas of the historical background of the aftermath of the Second World War and rebuilding of Europe; national political systems; issues and policies in Western European societies; European institutions and processes; and Europe's relations with the rest of the world.

• **An Introduction to the Modern Middle East** emphasizes core knowledge (including geography, Judaism, Christianity, Islam, ethnicity); nineteenth-century European impact; twentieth-century Western influences; World Wars I and II; new nations; social and cultural changes (1900-1960) and the Middle East from 1960 to present.

• **Human/Cultural Geography** includes the Earth and basic facts (coordinate systems, maps, physiography, atmosphere, soils and vegetation, water); culture and environment, spatial processes (social processes, modern economic systems, settlement patterns, political geography); and regional geography.

- **Rise and Fall of the Soviet Union** covers Russia under the Old Regime; the Revolutionary Period; New Economic Policy; Pre-war Stalinism; The Second World War; Post-war Stalinism; The Khrushchev Years; The Brezhnev Era; and reform and collapse.

- **A History of the Vietnam War** covers the history of the roots of the Vietnam War; the First Vietnam War (1946-1954); pre-war developments (1954-1963); American involvement in the Vietnam War; Tet (1968); Vietnamizing the War (1968-1973); Cambodia and Laos; peace; legacies and lessons.

- **The Civil War and Reconstruction** covers the Civil War from presecession (1861) through Reconstruction. It includes causes of the war; secession; Fort Sumter; the war in the east and in the west; major battles; the political situation; assassination of Lincoln; end of the Confederacy; and Reconstruction.

- **Foundations of Education** includes topics such as contemporary issues in education; past and current influences on education (philosophies, democratic ideals, social/economic influences); and the interrelationships between contemporary issues and influences.

- **Life-span Developmental Psychology** covers models and theories; methods of study; ethical issues; biological development; perception, learning and memory; cognition and language; social, emotional, and personality development; social behaviors, family life cycle, extrafamilial settings; singlehood and cohabitation; occupational development and retirement; adjustment to life stresses; and bereavement and loss.

- **Drug and Alcohol Abuse** includes such topics as drug use in society; classification of drugs; pharmacological principles; alcohol (types, effects of, alcoholism); general principles and use of sedative hypnotics, narcotic analgesics, stimulants, and hallucinogens; other drugs (inhalants, steroids); and prevention/treatment.

- **General Anthropology** deals with anthropology as a discipline; theoretical perspectives; physical anthropology; archaeology; social organization; economic organization; political organization; religion; and modernization and application of anthropology.

- **Introduction to Law Enforcement** includes topics such as history and professional movement of law enforcement; overview of the U.S. criminal justice system; police systems in the U.S.; police organization, management, and issues; and U.S. law and precedents.

- **Criminal Justice** deals with criminal behavior (crime in the U.S., theories of crime, types of crime); the criminal justice system (historical origins, legal foundations, due process); police; the court system (history and organization, adult court system, juvenile court, pre-trial and post-trial processes); and corrections.

- **Fundamentals of Counseling** covers historical development (significant influences and people); counselor roles and functions; the counseling relationship; and theoretical approaches to counseling.

Business
- **Principles of Finance** deals with financial statements and planning; time value of money; working capital management; valuation and characteristics; capital budgeting; cost of capital; risk and return; and international financial management. The use of a nonprogrammable, handheld calculator is permitted.

- **Principles of Financial Accounting** includes topics such as general concepts and principles, accounting cycle and classification; transaction analysis; accruals and deferrals; cash and internal control; current accounts; long- and short-term liabilities; capital stock; and financial statements. The use of a nonprogrammable, handheld calculator is permitted.

- **Human Resource Management** covers general employment issues; job analysis; training and development; performance appraisals; compensation issues; security issues; personnel legislation and regulation; labor relations and current issues; an overview of the Human Resource Management Field; Human Resource Planning; Staffing; training and development; compensation issues; safety and health; employee rights and discipline; employment law; labor relations and current issues and trends.

- **Organizational Behavior** deals with the study of organizational behavior (scientific approaches, research designs, data collection methods); individual processes and characteristics; interpersonal and group processes and characteristics; organizational processes and characteristics; and change and development processes.

- **Principles of Supervision** deals with the roles and responsibilities of the supervisor; management functions (planning, organization and staffing, directing at the supervisory level); and other topics (legal issues, stress management, union environments, quality concerns).

- **Business Law II** covers topics such as sales of goods; debtor and creditor relations; business organizations; property; and commercial paper.

- **Introduction to Computing** includes topics such as history and technological generations; hardware/software; applications to information technology; program development; data management; communications and connectivity; and computing and society. The use of a nonprogrammable, handheld calculator is permitted.

- **Management Information Systems** covers systems theory, analysis and design of systems, hardware and software; database management; telecommunications; management of the MIS functional area and informational support.

- **Introduction to Business** deals with economic issues affecting business; international business; government and business; forms of business ownership; small business, entrepreneurship and franchise; management process; human resource management; production and operations; marketing management; financial management; risk management and insurance; and management and information systems.

- **Money and Banking** covers the role and kinds of money; commercial banks and other financial intermediaries; central banking and the Federal Reserve system; money and macroeconomics activity; monetary policy in the U.S.; and the international monetary system.

- **Personal Finance** includes topics such as financial goals and values; budgeting; credit and debt; major purchases; taxes; insurance; investments; and retirement and estate planning. The use of auxiliary materials, such as calculators and slide rules, is NOT permitted.

- **Business Mathematics** deals with basic operations with integers, fractions, and decimals; round numbers; ratios; averages; business graphs; simple interest; compound interest and annuities; net pay and deductions; discounts and markups; depreciation and net worth; corporate securities; distribution of ownership; and stock and asset turnover.

Physical Science
• **Astronomy** covers the history of astronomy, celestial mechanics; celestial systems; astronomical instruments; the solar system; nature and evolution; the galaxy; the universe; determining astronomical distances; and life in the universe.

• **Here's to Your Health** covers mental health and behavior; human development and relationships; substance abuse; fitness and nutrition; risk factors, disease, and disease prevention; and safety, consumer awareness, and environmental concerns.

• **Environment and Humanity** deals with topics such as ecological concepts (ecosystems, global ecology, food chains and webs); environmental impacts; environmental management and conservation; and political processes and the future.

• **Principles of Physical Science I** includes physics: Newton's Laws of Motion; energy and momentum; thermodynamics; wave and optics; electricity and magnetism; chemistry: properties of matter; atomic theory and structure; and chemical reactions.

• **Physical Geology** covers Earth materials; igneous, sedimentary, and metamorphic rocks; surface processes (weathering, groundwater, glaciers, oceanic systems, deserts and winds, hydrologic cycle); internal Earth processes; and applications (mineral and energy resources, environmental geology).

Applied Technology
• **Technical Writing** covers topics such as theory and practice of technical writing; purpose, content, and organizational patterns of common types of technical documents; elements of various technical reports; and technical editing. Students have the option to write a short essay on one of the technical topics provided. Thomson Prometric will not score the essay; however, for determining the award of credit, a copy of the essay will be forwarded to the college or university you've designated along with the score report or transcript.

Humanities
• **Ethics in America** deals with ethical traditions (Greek views, Biblical traditions, moral law, consequential ethics, feminist ethics); ethical analysis of issues arising in interpersonal and personal-societal relationships and in professional and occupational roles; and relationships between ethical traditions and the ethical analysis of situations. Students have the option to write an essay to analyze a morally problematic situation in terms of issues relevant to a decision and arguments for alternative positions. Thomson Prometric will not score the essay; however, for determining the award of credit, a copy of the essay will be forwarded to the college or university you've designated along with the score report or transcript.

• **Introduction to World Religions** covers topics such as dimensions and approaches to religion; primal religions; Hinduism; Buddhism; Confucianism; Taoism; Judaism; Christianity; and Islam.

• **Principles of Public Speaking** consists of two parts: Part One consists of multiple-choice questions covering considerations of Principles of Public Speaking; audience analysis; purposes of speeches; structure/organization; content/supporting materials; research; language and style; delivery; communication apprehension; listening and feedback; and criticism and evaluation. Part Two requires the student to record an impromptu persuasive speech that will be scored.

FREQUENTLY ASKED QUESTIONS ABOUT DSSTs

In order to pass the test, must I study from one of the recommended references?
The recommended references are a listing of books that were being used as textbooks in college courses of the same or similar title at the time the test was developed. Appropriate textbooks for study are not limited to those listed in the fact sheet. If you wish to obtain study resources to prepare for the examination, you may reference either the current edition of the listed titles or textbooks currently used at a local college or university for the same class title. It is recommended that you reference more than one textbook on the topics outlined in the fact sheet. You should begin by checking textbook content against the content outline included on the front page of the DSST fact sheet before selecting textbooks that cover the text content from which to study. Textbooks may be found at the campus bookstore of a local college or university offering a course on the subject.

Is there a penalty for guessing on the tests?
There is no penalty for guessing on DSSTs, so you should mark an answer for each question.

How much time will I have to complete the test?
Many DSSTs can be completed within 90 minutes; however, additional time can be allowed if necessary.

What should I do if I find a test question irregularity?
Continue testing and then report the irregularity to the test administrator after the test. This may be done by asking that the test administrator note the irregularity on the Supervisor's Irregularity Report or you can write to Thomson Prometric, DSST Program, 2000 Lenox Drive, Third Floor, Lawrenceville, NJ 08648, and indicate the form and question number(s) or circumstances as well as your name and address.

When will I receive my score report?
Allow approximately four weeks from the date of testing to receive your score report. Allow six to eight weeks to receive a score report for the *Principles of Public Speaking* examination.

Will my test scores be released without my permission?
Your test score will not be released to anyone other than the school you designate on your answer sheet unless you write to us and ask us to send a transcript elsewhere. Instructions about how to do this can be found on your score report. Your scores may be used for research purposes, but individual scores are never made public nor are individuals identified if research findings are made public.

If I do not achieve a passing score on the test, how long must I wait until I can take the test again?
If you do not receive a score on the test that will enable you to obtain credit for the course, you may take the test again after six months (180 days). Please do not attempt to take the test before six months (180 days) have passed because you will receive a score report marked *invalid* and your test fee will not be refunded.

Can my test scores be canceled?

The test administrator is required to report any irregularities to Thomson Prometric. <u>The consequence of bringing unauthorized materials into the testing room, or giving or receiving help, will be the forfeiture of your test fee and the invalidation of test scores.</u> The DSST Program reserves the right to cancel scores and not issue score reports in such situations.

What can I do if I feel that my test scores were not accurately reported?

Thomson Prometric recognizes the extreme importance of test results to candidates and has a multi-step quality-control procedure to help ensure that reported scores are accurate. If you have reason to believe that your score(s) were not accurately reported, you may request to have your answer sheet reviewed and hand scored.

The fees for this service are:
- $20 fee if requested within six months of the test date
- $30 fee if requested more than six months from the test date
- $30 fee if a re-evaluation of the *Principles of Public Speaking* speech is requested

The fee for this service can be paid by credit card or by certified check or U.S. money order payable to Thomson Prometric. Submit your request for score verification along with the appropriate fee or credit card information (credit card number and expiration date) to Thomson Prometric, DSST Program, 2000 Lenox Drive, Third Floor, Lawrenceville, NJ 08648. Include your full name, the test title, the date you took the test, and your Social Security number. Candidates will be notified if a scoring discrepancy is discovered within four weeks of receipt of the request.

What does ACE recommendation mean?

The ACE recommendation is the minimum passing score recommended by the American Council on Education for any given test. It is equivalent to the average score of students in the DSST norming sample who received a grade of C for the course. Some schools require a score higher than the ACE recommendation.

Who is NLC?

National Learning Corporation (NLC) has been successfully preparing candidates for 40 years for over 5,000 exams. NLC publishes Passbook® study guides to help candidates prepare for all DANTES and CLEP exams and almost every other type of exam from high school through adult career.

Go to our website — www.passbooks.com — or call (800) 632-8888 for information about ordering our Passbooks.

To get detailed information on the DSST program and DSST preparation materials, visit www.getcollegecredit.com.

If you are interested in taking the DSST exams, call 877-471-9860 or e-mail pnj-dsst@thomson.com.

BUSINESS ETHICS AND SOCIETY

TEST INFORMATION

This test was developed to enable schools to award credit to students for knowledge equivalent to that learned by students taking the course. The school may choose to award college credit to the student based on the achievement of a passing score. The ultimate passing score for each examination is determined by the school. The school is provided with a recommended passing score established by a national committee of college faculty who teach these courses. The DSST program is approved by the American Council on Education (ACE), and the ACE provides both a recommended passing score and a recommended number of credits that could be awarded to successful students. Some schools set their own standards for awarding credit and may require a higher score than the ACE recommendation. Students should obtain this information from the institution from which they expect to receive credit.

CONTENT OUTLINE

The following is an outline of the content areas covered in the examination. The approximate percentage of the examination devoted to each content area is also noted.

I. Business Ethics – 5%
   a. Current state of business ethics
   b. Issues raised by various business scandals

II. Moral Philosophies and Business Ethics – 15%
   a. Kantian Ethics
   b. Kohlberg's model of cognitive moral development
   c. Mill's Utilitarianism
   d. Act and Rule Utilitarianism
   e. Social Contract

III. Social Responsibilities of a Business – 10%
   a. Can businesses have responsibility?
   b. Individual responsibilities within a business
   c. Global responsibilities of a business

IV. Regulation of Business – 10%
   a. Theoretical issues
   b. Consequences

V. Employer-Employee Relations – 10%
   a. Confidentiality and whistle-blowing
   b. Discrimination and affirmative action
   c. Sexual harassment
   d. Duties of corporate officers
   e. Labor relations

VI. Ethics of Information – 10%
   a. Marketing and advertising
   b. Bluffing and spying
   c. Privacy issues/concerns
   d. Control of proprietary information

VII. Ethics in International Business – 10%
   a. Corporate citizenship in a global economy
   b. Ethics in transnational corporations
   c. Overseas work assignments and outsourcing
   d. Ethical standards in different countries

VIII. Corporations and Stakeholders – 10%
   a. Relationship with stockholders
   b. Relationship with employees
   c. The corporation within the community and the public good
   d. Corporations and consumers

From the official announcement for educational purposes

IX. Ecology and Global Business – 10%
a. Sustainable business growth and the environment
b. Corporate responsibility for the environment

X. Business and Government – 10%
a. Corporate relationships with political leaders (positive and negative)
b. Governmental control over business activities
c. Business, government, and the law

REFERENCES
The following references were used to create exam questions and may be useful as study materials. You are not allowed to use these references in the testing center.

1. *Business Ethics – Ethical Decision Making and Cases*, 7th Edition, 2008, Houghton Mifflin Company, 222 Berkely Street, Boston, MA 02116 (www.hmco.com).
2. *Ethics and the Conduct of Business,* 6th Edition, 2009, Pearson Education, Upper Saddle River, New Jersey (www.pearsonhighered.com).
3. *Business and Society – Shareholders, Ethics, and Public Policy*, 12th Edition, McGraw-Hill, 2008, 1221 Avenue of the Americas, New York, NY 10020 (www.mcgraw-hill.com)
4. *Business and Society – Ethics and Stakeholder Management*, 7th edition, 2009, South-Western Cengage Learning, 5191 Natorp Boulevard, Mason, OH. 45040 (www.cengage.com)

SAMPLE QUESTIONS
All test questions are in a multiple-choice format, with one correct answer and three incorrect options. You may want to review these samples for the type of questions that may appear on the exam.

1. Business ethics deals with
    a. morality
    b. ethnicity
    c. economics
    d. philanthropy

2. What contemporary business practice is most similar to utilitarian reasoning?
    a. Truth in lending
    b. Cost-benefit analysis
    c. Truth in advertising
    d. The customer is always right

3. Which form of "bribe" offered to an official in a foreign country is understood to be acceptable under the Foreign Corrupt Practices Act of 1977?
    a. Payments made to police officers to get them to overlook minor infractions
    b. Payments made to judges to get them to rule against guilty parties
    c. Payments made to bureaucrats to get them to expedite their assigned tasks
    d. Payments made to lawmakers to get them to vote for favorable legislation

4. According to Boatwright, which of the following could best describe a living wage?
    a. The wages offered by the employer
    b. The wage at which an employee will work
    c. A wage that is considered poverty level income
    d. Wages that enables a worker to support a family with dignity

5. An emerging view of corporate whistle-blowing practices regards them as justified, particularly when an employee's
    a. duty of loyalty outweighs obligations of confidentiality
    b. obligation under the law outweighs the right to privacy
    c. right to security outweighs the responsibility to prevent harm
    d. responsibility to the public outweighs duties to an employer

6. Under the Equal Employment Opportunity Commission's definition of sexual harassment, which of the following is a category of harassment?
   a. Glass ceiling
   b. Quid pro quo
   c. Absenteeism
   d. Comparable worth

7. Which act provides whistle-blowers with the greatest protection?
   a. False Claims Act
   b. Sarbanes-Oxley Act
   c. The Civil Rights Act
   d. The Government Protection Act

8. Byron has started a new position as an accountant at company XYZ. Company XYZ maintains medical records on employees in order to administer benefit plans or to monitor occupational health and safety. No health and safety issues are associated with Byron's position.
   Which of the following individuals should have access and is justified in obtaining Byron's medical information?
   a. Tara, the CEO of company XYZ, who has access to all of the medical records
   b. Heather, the HR generalist, who administers the company health insurance plan
   c. Bill, Byron's first-line supervisor, who will use the information for Byron's performance evaluation
   d. Tom, Byron's supervisor and vice president of the division, who will use the information to determine future promotions

9. A corporation may be excused from the requirements of the Worker Adjustment and Retraining Notification Act (WARN) if immediate layoffs were
   a. accompanied by outplacement benefit programs
   b. a response to declining levels of employee productivity
   c. necessary as a result of unforeseen business circumstances
   d. achieved through the elimination of an entire business division

10. Sustainable development requires that human society use natural resources at a rate that can be continued over a(n)
    a. indefinite period
    b. protected period
    c. renewable period
    d. sustainable period

Answers to sample questions: 1-A; 2-B; 3-C ; 4-D; 5-D; 6-B; 7-B; 8-B; 9-C; 10-A.

CREDIT RECOMMENDATIONS

The Center for Adult Learning and Educational Credentials of the American Council on Education (ACE) has reviewed and evaluated the DSST test development process for and content of this exam. It has made the following recommendations:

Area or Course Equivalent	Business Ethics & Society
Level	Upper-level baccalaureate
Amount of Credit	Three (3) semester hours
Source	ACE Commission on Education Credit and Credentials

It is advisable that schools develop a consistent policy about awarding credit based on scores from this test and that the policy be reviewed periodically. Prometric will be happy to help schools in this effort.

HOW TO TAKE A TEST

You have studied long, hard and conscientiously.

With your official admission card in hand, and your heart pounding, you have been admitted to the examination room.

You note that there are several hundred other applicants in the examination room waiting to take the same test.

They all appear to be equally well prepared.

You know that nothing but your best effort will suffice. The "moment of truth" is at hand: you now have to demonstrate objectively, in writing, your knowledge of content and your understanding of subject matter.

You are fighting the most important battle of your life—to pass and/or score high on an examination which will determine your career and provide the economic basis for your livelihood.

What extra, special things should you know and should you do in taking the examination?

I. YOU MUST PASS AN EXAMINATION

A. WHAT EVERY CANDIDATE SHOULD KNOW
Examination applicants often ask us for help in preparing for the written test. What can I study in advance? What kinds of questions will be asked? How will the test be given? How will the papers be graded?

B. HOW ARE EXAMS DEVELOPED?
Examinations are carefully written by trained technicians who are specialists in the field known as "psychological measurement," in consultation with recognized authorities in the field of work that the test will cover. These experts recommend the subject matter areas or skills to be tested; only those knowledges or skills important to your success on the job are included. The most reliable books and source materials available are used as references. Together, the experts and technicians judge the difficulty level of the questions.
Test technicians know how to phrase questions so that the problem is clearly stated. Their ethics do not permit "trick" or "catch" questions. Questions may have been tried out on sample groups, or subjected to statistical analysis, to determine their usefulness.
Written tests are often used in combination with performance tests, ratings of training and experience, and oral interviews. All of these measures combine to form the best-known means of finding the right person for the right job.

II. HOW TO PASS THE WRITTEN TEST

A. BASIC STEPS

1) Study the announcement

How, then, can you know what subjects to study? Our best answer is: "Learn as much as possible about the class of positions for which you've applied." The exam will test the knowledge, skills and abilities needed to do the work.

Your most valuable source of information about the position you want is the official exam announcement. This announcement lists the training and experience qualifications. Check these standards and apply only if you come reasonably close to meeting them. Many jurisdictions preview the written test in the exam announcement by including a section called "Knowledge and Abilities Required," "Scope of the Examination," or some similar heading. Here you will find out specifically what fields will be tested.

2) Choose appropriate study materials

If the position for which you are applying is technical or advanced, you will read more advanced, specialized material. If you are already familiar with the basic principles of your field, elementary textbooks would waste your time. Concentrate on advanced textbooks and technical periodicals. Think through the concepts and review difficult problems in your field.

These are all general sources. You can get more ideas on your own initiative, following these leads. For example, training manuals and publications of the government agency which employs workers in your field can be useful, particularly for technical and professional positions. A letter or visit to the government department involved may result in more specific study suggestions, and certainly will provide you with a more definite idea of the exact nature of the position you are seeking.

3) Study this book!

III. KINDS OF TESTS

Tests are used for purposes other than measuring knowledge and ability to perform specified duties. For some positions, it is equally important to test ability to make adjustments to new situations or to profit from training. In others, basic mental abilities not dependent on information are essential. Questions which test these things may not appear as pertinent to the duties of the position as those which test for knowledge and information. Yet they are often highly important parts of a fair examination. For very general questions, it is almost impossible to help you direct your study efforts. What we can do is to point out some of the more common of these general abilities needed in public service positions and describe some typical questions.

1) General information

Broad, general information has been found useful for predicting job success in some kinds of work. This is tested in a variety of ways, from vocabulary lists to questions about current events. Basic background in some field of work, such as sociology or economics, may be sampled in a group of questions. Often these are principles which have become familiar to most persons through exposure rather than through formal training. It is difficult to advise you how to study for these questions; being alert to the world around you is our best suggestion.

2) Verbal ability
An example of an ability needed in many positions is verbal or language ability. Verbal ability is, in brief, the ability to use and understand words. Vocabulary and grammar tests are typical measures of this ability. Reading comprehension or paragraph interpretation questions are common in many kinds of civil service tests. You are given a paragraph of written material and asked to find its central meaning.

IV. KINDS OF QUESTIONS

1. Multiple-choice Questions
Most popular of the short-answer questions is the "multiple choice" or "best answer" question. It can be used, for example, to test for factual knowledge, ability to solve problems or judgment in meeting situations found at work.
A multiple-choice question is normally one of three types:
- It can begin with an incomplete statement followed by several possible endings. You are to find the one ending which best completes the statement, although some of the others may not be entirely wrong.
- It can also be a complete statement in the form of a question which is answered by choosing one of the statements listed.
- It can be in the form of a problem – again you select the best answer.

Here is an example of a multiple-choice question with a discussion which should give you some clues as to the method for choosing the right answer:

When an employee has a complaint about his assignment, the action which will best help him overcome his difficulty is to
    A. discuss his difficulty with his coworkers
    B. take the problem to the head of the organization
    C. take the problem to the person who gave him the assignment
    D. say nothing to anyone about his complaint

In answering this question, you should study each of the choices to find which is best. Consider choice "A" – Certainly an employee may discuss his complaint with fellow employees, but no change or improvement can result, and the complaint remains unresolved. Choice "B" is a poor choice since the head of the organization probably does not know what assignment you have been given, and taking your problem to him is known as "going over the head" of the supervisor. The supervisor, or person who made the assignment, is the person who can clarify it or correct any injustice. Choice "C" is, therefore, correct. To say nothing, as in choice "D," is unwise. Supervisors have and interest in knowing the problems employees are facing, and the employee is seeking a solution to his problem.

2. True/False

3. Matching Questions
Matching an answer from a column of choices within another column.

V. RECORDING YOUR ANSWERS

Computer terminals are used more and more today for many different kinds of exams.

For an examination with very few applicants, you may be told to record your answers in the test booklet itself. Separate answer sheets are much more common. If this separate answer sheet is to be scored by machine – and this is often the case – it is highly important that you mark your answers correctly in order to get credit.

VI. BEFORE THE TEST

YOUR PHYSICAL CONDITION IS IMPORTANT

If you are not well, you can't do your best work on tests. If you are half asleep, you can't do your best either. Here are some tips:

1) Get about the same amount of sleep you usually get. Don't stay up all night before the test, either partying or worrying—DON'T DO IT!
2) If you wear glasses, be sure to wear them when you go to take the test. This goes for hearing aids, too.
3) If you have any physical problems that may keep you from doing your best, be sure to tell the person giving the test. If you are sick or in poor health, you relay cannot do your best on any test. You can always come back and take the test some other time.

Common sense will help you find procedures to follow to get ready for an examination. Too many of us, however, overlook these sensible measures. Indeed, nervousness and fatigue have been found to be the most serious reasons why applicants fail to do their best on civil service tests. Here is a list of reminders:

- Begin your preparation early – Don't wait until the last minute to go scurrying around for books and materials or to find out what the position is all about.
- Prepare continuously – An hour a night for a week is better than an all-night cram session. This has been definitely established. What is more, a night a week for a month will return better dividends than crowding your study into a shorter period of time.
- Locate the place of the exam – You have been sent a notice telling you when and where to report for the examination. If the location is in a different town or otherwise unfamiliar to you, it would be well to inquire the best route and learn something about the building.
- Relax the night before the test – Allow your mind to rest. Do not study at all that night. Plan some mild recreation or diversion; then go to bed early and get a good night's sleep.
- Get up early enough to make a leisurely trip to the place for the test – This way unforeseen events, traffic snarls, unfamiliar buildings, etc. will not upset you.
- Dress comfortably – A written test is not a fashion show. You will be known by number and not by name, so wear something comfortable.
- Leave excess paraphernalia at home – Shopping bags and odd bundles will get in your way. You need bring only the items mentioned in the official notice you received; usually everything you need is provided. Do not bring reference books to the exam. They will only confuse those last minutes and be taken away from you when in the test room.

- Arrive somewhat ahead of time – If because of transportation schedules you must get there very early, bring a newspaper or magazine to take your mind off yourself while waiting.
- Locate the examination room – When you have found the proper room, you will be directed to the seat or part of the room where you will sit. Sometimes you are given a sheet of instructions to read while you are waiting. Do not fill out any forms until you are told to do so; just read them and be prepared.
- Relax and prepare to listen to the instructions
- If you have any physical problem that may keep you from doing your best, be sure to tell the test administrator. If you are sick or in poor health, you really cannot do your best on the exam. You can come back and take the test some other time.

VII. AT THE TEST

The day of the test is here and you have the test booklet in your hand. The temptation to get going is very strong. Caution! There is more to success than knowing the right answers. You must know how to identify your papers and understand variations in the type of short-answer question used in this particular examination. Follow these suggestions for maximum results from your efforts:

1) Cooperate with the monitor

The test administrator has a duty to create a situation in which you can be as much at ease as possible. He will give instructions, tell you when to begin, check to see that you are marking your answer sheet correctly, and so on. He is not there to guard you, although he will see that your competitors do not take unfair advantage. He wants to help you do your best.

2) Listen to all instructions

Don't jump the gun! Wait until you understand all directions. In most civil service tests you get more time than you need to answer the questions. So don't be in a hurry. Read each word of instructions until you clearly understand the meaning. Study the examples, listen to all announcements and follow directions. Ask questions if you do not understand what to do.

3) Identify your papers

Civil service exams are usually identified by number only. You will be assigned a number; you must not put your name on your test papers. Be sure to copy your number correctly. Since more than one exam may be given, copy your exact examination title.

4) Plan your time

Unless you are told that a test is a "speed" or "rate of work" test, speed itself is usually not important. Time enough to answer all the questions will be provided, but this does not mean that you have all day. An overall time limit has been set. Divide the total time (in minutes) by the number of questions to determine the approximate time you have for each question.

5) Do not linger over difficult questions

If you come across a difficult question, mark it with a paper clip (useful to have along) and come back to it when you have been through the booklet. One caution if you do this – be sure to skip a number on your answer sheet as well. Check often to be sure that you have not lost your place and that you are marking in the row numbered the same as the question you are answering.

6) Read the questions

Be sure you know what the question asks! Many capable people are unsuccessful because they failed to read the questions correctly.

7) Answer all questions

Unless you have been instructed that a penalty will be deducted for incorrect answers, it is better to guess than to omit a question.

8) Speed tests

It is often better NOT to guess on speed tests. It has been found that on timed tests people are tempted to spend the last few seconds before time is called in marking answers at random – without even reading them – in the hope of picking up a few extra points. To discourage this practice, the instructions may warn you that your score will be "corrected" for guessing. That is, a penalty will be applied. The incorrect answers will be deducted from the correct ones, or some other penalty formula will be used.

9) Review your answers

If you finish before time is called, go back to the questions you guessed or omitted to give them further thought. Review other answers if you have time.

10) Return your test materials

If you are ready to leave before others have finished or time is called, take ALL your materials to the monitor and leave quietly. Never take any test material with you. The monitor can discover whose papers are not complete, and taking a test booklet may be grounds for disqualification.

VIII. EXAMINATION TECHNIQUES

1) Read the general instructions carefully. These are usually printed on the first page of the exam booklet. As a rule, these instructions refer to the timing of the examination; the fact that you should not start work until the signal and must stop work at a signal, etc. If there are any special instructions, such as a choice of questions to be answered, make sure that you note this instruction carefully.

2) When you are ready to start work on the examination, that is as soon as the signal has been given, read the instructions to each question booklet, underline any key words or phrases, such as least, best, outline, describe and the like. In this way you will tend to answer as requested rather than discover on reviewing your paper that you listed without describing, that you selected the worst choice rather than the best choice, etc.

3) If the examination is of the objective or multiple-choice type – that is, each question will also give a series of possible answers: A, B, C or D, and you are called upon to select the best answer and write the letter next to that answer on your answer paper – it is advisable to start answering each question in turn. There may be anywhere from 50 to 100 such questions in the three or four hours allotted and you can see how much time would be taken if you read through all the questions before beginning to answer any. Furthermore, if you

come across a question or group of questions which you know would be difficult to answer, it would undoubtedly affect your handling of all the other questions.

4) If the examination is of the essay type and contains but a few questions, it is a moot point as to whether you should read all the questions before starting to answer any one. Of course, if you are given a choice – say five out of seven and the like – then it is essential to read all the questions so you can eliminate the two that are most difficult. If, however, you are asked to answer all the questions, there may be danger in trying to answer the easiest one first because you may find that you will spend too much time on it. The best technique is to answer the first question, then proceed to the second, etc.

5) Time your answers. Before the exam begins, write down the time it started, then add the time allowed for the examination and write down the time it must be completed, then divide the time available somewhat as follows:
    - If 3-1/2 hours are allowed, that would be 210 minutes. If you have 80 objective-type questions, that would be an average of 2-1/2 minutes per question. Allow yourself no more than 2 minutes per question, or a total of 160 minutes, which will permit about 50 minutes to review.
    - If for the time allotment of 210 minutes there are 7 essay questions to answer, that would average about 30 minutes a question. Give yourself only 25 minutes per question so that you have about 35 minutes to review.

6) The most important instruction is to read each question and make sure you know what is wanted. The second most important instruction is to time yourself properly so that you answer every question. The third most important instruction is to answer every question. Guess if you have to but include something for each question. Remember that you will receive no credit for a blank and will probably receive some credit if you write something in answer to an essay question. If you guess a letter – say "B" for a multiple-choice question – you may have guessed right. If you leave a blank as an answer to a multiple-choice question, the examiners may respect your feelings but it will not add a point to your score. Some exams may penalize you for wrong answers, so in such cases only, you may not want to guess unless you have some basis for your answer.

7) Suggestions
    a. Objective-type questions
        1. Examine the question booklet for proper sequence of pages and questions
        2. Read all instructions carefully
        3. Skip any question which seems too difficult; return to it after all other questions have been answered
        4. Apportion your time properly; do not spend too much time on any single question or group of questions
        5. Note and underline key words – all, most, fewest, least, best, worst, same, opposite, etc.
        6. Pay particular attention to negatives
        7. Note unusual option, e.g., unduly long, short, complex, different or similar in content to the body of the question
        8. Observe the use of "hedging" words – probably, may, most likely, etc.

9. Make sure that your answer is put next to the same number as the question
10. Do not second-guess unless you have good reason to believe the second answer is definitely more correct
11. Cross out original answer if you decide another answer is more accurate; do not erase until you are ready to hand your paper in
12. Answer all questions; guess unless instructed otherwise
13. Leave time for review

   b. Essay questions
1. Read each question carefully
2. Determine exactly what is wanted. Underline key words or phrases.
3. Decide on outline or paragraph answer
4. Include many different points and elements unless asked to develop any one or two points or elements
5. Show impartiality by giving pros and cons unless directed to select one side only
6. Make and write down any assumptions you find necessary to answer the questions
7. Watch your English, grammar, punctuation and choice of words
8. Time your answers; don't crowd material

8) Answering the essay question

Most essay questions can be answered by framing the specific response around several key words or ideas. Here are a few such key words or ideas:

M's: manpower, materials, methods, money, management
P's: purpose, program, policy, plan, procedure, practice, problems, pitfalls, personnel, public relations

  a. Six basic steps in handling problems:
1. Preliminary plan and background development
2. Collect information, data and facts
3. Analyze and interpret information, data and facts
4. Analyze and develop solutions as well as make recommendations
5. Prepare report and sell recommendations
6. Install recommendations and follow up effectiveness

  b. Pitfalls to avoid
1. Taking things for granted – A statement of the situation does not necessarily imply that each of the elements is necessarily true; for example, a complaint may be invalid and biased so that all that can be taken for granted is that a complaint has been registered
2. Considering only one side of a situation – Wherever possible, indicate several alternatives and then point out the reasons you selected the best one
3. Failing to indicate follow up – Whenever your answer indicates action on your part, make certain that you will take proper follow-up action to see how successful your recommendations, procedures or actions turn out to be
4. Taking too long in answering any single question – Remember to time your answers properly

EXAMINATION SECTION

EXAMINATION SECTION
TEST 1

DIRECTIONS: Each question or incomplete statement is followed by several suggested answers or completions. Select the one that BEST answers the question or completes the statement. *PRINT THE LETTER OF THE CORRECT ANSWER IN THE SPACE AT THE RIGHT.*

1. In the developing field of human gene therapy, which is generally considered the MOST ethically sound end for treatment?   1.____

    A. Therapeutic repair
    B. Alternative creation
    C. Composite trait selection
    D. Subjective enhancement

2. Which of the following was NOT a belief embraced by the American counter-cultural movement of the 1960s?   2.____

    A. The placement of sensory experience ahead of conceptual knowledge
    B. Existential emphasis on being rather than doing
    C. The rejection of mastery over nature
    D. Valuing detachment, objectivity, and noninvolvement as methods for finding truth

3. According to inquiries of American workers, APPROXIMATELY what percentage of people claim to be currently performing at the level that demonstrates the full range of their capabilities?   3.____

    A. 10   B. 25   C. 50   D. 75

4. Currently, which is NOT known to be an element of the most effective welfare/entitlement programs in the United States?   4.____

    A. Small offices with close ties to communities and local employers
    B. A flat bureaucratic hierarchy with a limited number of levels
    C. Cautious, custodial leadership with fixed policies and procedures
    D. Little political input from local or state politicians

5. MOST professional codes of ethics   5.____

    A. embody a broad picture of expected moral character
    B. are voluntary
    C. provide specific guidance for action in situations
    D. are decided by objective ethicists outside of the profession

6. Currently, the MOST important factor determining a child's success in an American school is the   6.____

    A. student's racial/ethnic background
    B. student's financial standing
    C. education level of the student's parents
    D. student's sense of responsibility for his/her performance

7. Since the 1920s, the research of advertising companies has revealed that the most effective ads generally produce what sort of response from potential consumers?

    A. The belief that the product or service is of high quality
    B. A strong emotional reaction
    C. The belief that the product or service is economical
    D. A desire for time-saving convenience

8. Of the following, the LEAST important determining factor for an individual's personal ethic is

    A. reason   B. religion   C. emotion   D. law

9. Each of the factors below has contributed to the change in American political campaign ethics EXCEPT

    A. party reforms devaluing individual voters
    B. technological innovations
    C. lengthening campaigns
    D. shifting demographics

10. Contemporary broadcasts in American television are designed to promote each of the following conditions among viewers EXCEPT

    A. awareness
    C. interest
    B. understanding response
    D. knowledge

11. To early American Calvinists, the PRIMARY spiritual/religious purpose of work was to

    A. secure a place with God in the afterlife
    B. produce material comforts
    C. avoid vacant time that might inspire evil thoughts
    D. to assure onself that he/she was a member of the elected inhabitants of God's kingdom

12. In questioning the moral rules that apply in any given situation, an individual is operating on the _____ level in the determination of what is good or right.

    A. expressive-evocative
    C. ethical
    B. moral
    D. post-ethical

13. Which of the four guiding principles of modern medicine specifically resulted from the knowledge of experiments that were performed on unknowing subjects?

    A. Beneficence
    C. Justice
    B. Nonmaleficence
    D. Autonomy

14. The majority of American citizens currently view employment in terms of all of the following EXCEPT

    A. status
    B. expression of self-interest
    C. social obligation
    D. economic necessity

15. Which of the following is LEAST likely, in the current American work environment, to improve standards for American workers? 15.____

    A. Making employees personally accountable for job performance
    B. Assigning workers a role in planning tasks
    C. Division of labor into more specialized roles
    D. Direct feedback from consumers to workers

16. According to most contemporary opinion polls, which of the following characteristics is considered to be LEAST important to the effectiveness of a public official? 16.____

    A. Prudence   B. Practical wisdom
    C. Honesty   D. Courage

17. Generally, the current social trends in American demographics show that most people value employment primarily for each of the following reasons EXCEPT 17.____

    A. economic benefits
    B. avoiding the embarrassment of public assistance
    C. the inherent morality in work and labor
    D. peripheral benefits such as health care and insurance

18. The contemporary revolution in the communication media, especially broadcast, is generally thought to be a product of 18.____

    A. the way in which most American lives are lived
    B. the way most Americans believe their lives should be lived
    C. fictions of life that are contrived by a limited corps of media personnel
    D. nostalgic reflections on life as it used to be

19. The pattern of distribution reflecting the movement of the American personal work ethic throughout the country's early population is from the 19.____

    A. lower class upward
    B. upper class downward
    C. middle class to the lower class
    D. middle class into both the upper and lower classes

20. Generally, in the latter part of the twentieth century, M.B.A.-trained managers increased short-term profits in large corporations (such as steel and automobile industries) through each of the following practices EXCEPT 20.____

    A. denial of funds for research and product development
    B. sacrificing product quality
    C. elimination of funds for modernization of equipment and facilities
    D. widespread cuts in labor wages

21. According to the utilitarian school of ethics, the MOST reliable source of moral standards in any society is 21.____

    A. the laws formulated by a democratically-elected government
    B. the discourse of an elite corps of intellectual moralists
    C. the opinions and convictions of the majority
    D. a randomly chosen individual citizen

22. Generally, the field of bioethics began with the _____ principle as its primary concern. 22._____

    A. quality of life
    B. cost-efficiency of individual treatment
    C. collective good of individual treatment
    D. sanctity of life

23. After World War I, which of the following conditions did NOT contribute to a change in the American work ethic? 23._____

    A. Widespread desire for emotional release
    B. Material prosperity
    C. A slackening sense of religious obligation
    D. Production of nonessential *leisure* products such as radios and automobiles

24. The GREATEST source of income for most members of the House and Senate is from 24._____

    A. government salary
    B. outside jobs
    C. unearned income from dividends and investments
    D. honoraria for speaking engagements

25. In general, the effect of American television news broadcasts in recent years has shifted citizen involvement in government from 25._____

    A. response to initiation
    B. detachment to involvement
    C. crisis to policy-making
    D. action to reaction

KEY (CORRECT ANSWERS)

1.	A	11.	D
2.	D	12.	C
3.	B	13.	D
4.	C	14.	C
5.	A	15.	C
6.	D	16.	C
7.	B	17.	C
8.	D	18.	C
9.	A	19.	D
10.	B	20.	D

21. C
22. D
23. C
24. C
25. D

TEST 2

DIRECTIONS: Each question or incomplete statement is followed by several suggested answers or completions. Select the one that BEST answers the question or completes the statement. *PRINT THE LETTER OF THE CORRECT ANSWER IN THE SPACE AT THE RIGHT.*

1. Which of the following was NOT an element that contributed directly to the growth of the work ethic in America's early agricultural society?

    A. Abundant, easily-tapped natural resources
    B. A free-enterprise economy
    C. Immediate, tangible rewards for labor
    D. Religious freedom

2. The growth of American manufacturing companies generally resulted in each of the following conditions EXCEPT

    A. swelling of corporate bureaucracies
    B. decreased pressure on management personnel
    C. expansion of work responsibilities for laborers
    D. discouragement of competition from developing companies

3. Which of the following duties is NOT considered to be an appropriate use of personal staff by Congressional members?

    A. Coordinating meetings
    B. Answering correspondence
    C. Writing speeches and correspondence
    D. Distributing campaign literature

4. The trend in current American education, especially at the university level, teaches ethics in a social context that promotes

    A. the development of individual virtue
    B. ethical relativism
    C. ethics are most important in the professional arena
    D. public policy as the primary agent of principles

5. Currently, the function of the American health care industry that would serve the population MOST effectively and inexpensively is perceived to be

    A. expansion of emergency services
    B. increased specialization
    C. prevention of health crises
    D. curing afflicted individuals

6. In recent years, the majority of non-partisan social policy analysts attribute the persistence of poverty in the United States to

    A. social barriers
    B. economic injustice
    C. systematic discrimination
    D. lack of attractive work incentives

7. Which of the following is NOT viewed by many physicians and bioethicists as an inevitable result of the unfolding knowledge of the human genome?

    A. The patenting of human genes
    B. An explosion in legal costs
    C. An increased abortion rate
    D. The proliferation of new genetic diseases

8. Which is NOT considered to be one of the primary ethical standards against which public behavior is to be judged in a democratic society?

    A. Rationality B. Personal convictions
    C. Democratic process D. Choice

9. Generally, the legal precedents in the United States have been MOST likely to award decision-making rights concerning a child to the _____ mother.

    A. genetic B. gestational
    C. social D. spiritual

10. During which decade did the installation of computer-programmed machinery begin to replace the human skill requirement in many industrial jobs?

    A. 1960s B. 1970s C. 1980s D. 1990s

11. Which of the following is NOT a factor contributing to the Federal government's inability to set behavior standards for the recipients of its entitlement programs?

    A. Limitations of Federal constitutional authority
    B. Implementation difficulties
    C. The differing and conflicting approaches of policy analysts
    D. Lack of capital to transform current programs

12. In which American service industry are ethical codes considered to be voluntary?

    A. Legal representation
    B. Health care
    C. Financial/tax services
    D. Radio and television broadcasting

13. Which ethical code would MOST likely condemn the distribution of disinfected hypodermic syringes to known drug addicts in order to prevent the spread of disease?

    A. Teleological B. Deontological
    C. Utilitarian D. Existential

14. In contemporary American politics, the power of a campaign is rooted in

    A. facts B. issues
    C. causes and effects D. stories and rites

15. As they were originally designed, affirmative action practices in America were intended to promote

    A. the establishment of racial quotas in hiring practices
    B. active recruitment of qualified applicants from historically excluded groups

C. lowering of hiring and acceptance standards among certain groups
D. a workforce and student population that was proportionally matched to the population at large

16. The American work ethic received its GREATEST blow among educated professionals (professors, physicians, therapists) from

    A. the human potential movement in American psychology
    B. the counter-cultural movement among American students
    C. lack of pride in work results
    D. the entertainment industry

17. The term for the shared values of a political democracy is

    A. over-ethic   B. public interest
    C. public opinion   D. policy

18. In general, the use of television as a medium for campaign broadcasting in the United States is considered to have resulted in each of the following EXCEPT

    A. decreased voter turnout
    B. longer speeches by candidates
    C. increased cynicism
    D. lower levels of political knowledge

19. In a democratic society, the _____ is usually considered to be the agent of ethical conduct.

    A. individual citizen   B. elected official
    C. academic scholar   D. information media

20. In the last few decades, personal staff work forces hired by House and Senate members have

    A. decreased by about half
    B. remained about the same size
    C. doubled
    D. tripled

21. Which body of ethical thought has its roots MOST firmly in American traditions?

    A. Phenomenology   B. Utilitarianism
    C. Pragmatism   D. Existentialism

22. Most ethical codes for physicians hold each of the following conditions to be signs of incompetence for informed consent in patients EXCEPT the inability to

    A. offer risk/benefit reasons
    B. communicate or articulate specific reasons
    C. grasp the situation
    D. reach a reasonable decision

23. Amzong typical American low-wage workers, the GREATEST sense of personal shame results from 23.____

    A. failure to meet social obligations
    B. poor performance on the job
    C. low status of individual position
    D. poor living conditions

24. Which ethical code is based on the possible good produced by behaviors? 24.____

    A. Deontological   B. Epistemological
    C. Teleological   D. Existential

25. The PRIMARY purpose for sperm banks in the United States is shifting toward 25.____

    A. a private industry for trait selection
    B. public storage to be accessed by women who want to bear children
    C. donation for research purposes
    D. storage for men who want to insure their own ability to father children in the future

---

KEY (CORRECT ANSWERS)

1. D   11. D
2. C   12. D
3. D   13. B
4. D   14. D
5. C   15. B

6. D   16. A
7. C   17. B
8. B   18. B
9. B   19. A
10. C   20. D

21. C
22. B
23. C
24. C
25. A

TEST 3

DIRECTIONS: Each question or incomplete statement is followed by several suggested answers or completions. Select the one that BEST answers the question or completes the statement. *PRINT THE LETTER OF THE CORRECT ANSWER IN THE SPACE AT THE RIGHT.*

1. The trend in the American health care industry is seen to have shifted its emphasis toward

    A. research
    B. therapeutic intervention
    C. prevention of disease
    D. curing afflicted individuals

    1.____

2. In which type of government are ethical concerns MOST prominently at issue?

    A. Monarchy
    B. Totalitarian dictatorship
    C. Democracy
    D. Collectivist/communist

    2.____

3. The professional campaigners who currently dominate the American political scene view the American public as capable of responsibly judging all but _____ in a candidate.

    A. charisma
    B. image
    C. reliability in performing public duties
    D. current stance on specific issues

    3.____

4. What was the initial, primary purpose for sperm banks in the United States?

    A. A private industry for trait selection
    B. Public storage to be accessed by women who want to bear children
    C. Donation for research purposes
    D. Storage for men who wanted to insure their own ability to father children in the future

    4.____

5. Which of the following conditions was NOT responsible for the severe damage inflicted upon the American work ethic in the mid-1980s?

    A. Fractionation of jobs
    B. Intense skill requirements in manufacturing jobs
    C. Dominant values of pleasure and entertainment
    D. Emphasis on short-term profits

    5.____

6. In mainstream television news broadcasts in the United States, video footage is increasingly used PRIMARILY to

    A. illustrate a news story
    B. slow the pace of a broadcast
    C. substitute for narrative and analysis
    D. provide facts and statistics

    6.____

9

7. Generally, in the late twentieth century, the trend in American social policy shifted responsibility toward which element of society?

   A. Family
   B. Government
   C. Smaller communities
   D. The individual

8. During which decade did alarm from corporate managers about the threat of foreign competition FIRST become widespread?

   A. 1950s   B. 1960s   C. 1970s   D. 1980s

9. Which characteristic is an example of the *golden mean* advocated by traditional codes of ethics?

   A. Humility
   B. Modesty
   C. Pride
   D. Arrogance

10. In American politics, which of the following factors is NOT a reason for the population's difficulty in judging a candidate's ethical competency?

    A. Length of campaigns making occasions for assessment highly variable
    B. Availability of printed media
    C. Most candidates and campaigners viewing ethical standards as situational
    D. Increasingly shorter speeches and interviews

11. The field of bioethics has gradually shifted toward the _____ principle as its PRIMARY concern.

    A. quality of life
    B. cost-efficiency of individual treatment
    C. collective good of individual treatment
    D. sanctity of life

12. Beginning in the early twentieth century, which pattern of activity was considered MOST desirable to American workers?

    A. Sustained work interrupted by brief periods of vigorous recreation
    B. Long periods of leisure interrupted by necessary work tasks
    C. Sustained work interrupted by brief periods of idle resting time
    D. Sustained religious observance interrupted by brief periods of intense labor

13. The distribution of condoms among high school students in order to prevent the spread of disease would be MOST effectively justified by which ethical code?

    A. Deontological
    B. Teleological
    C. Phenomenological
    D. Existential

14. In contemporary American society, the vast majority of abortions are the result of indications from _____ concerns.

    A. sociological
    B. maternal
    C. fetal
    D. humanitarian

15. Beginning in the 1920s, the American advertising industry found that consumers were influenced PRIMARILY by appeals to

    A. vanity   B. sex drive   C. reason   D. hunger

16. Which of the following is a belief embraced by the American counter-cultural movement of the 1960s?

    A. Rejection of rules that interfere with natural function and expression
    B. Devaluing the search for truth through experience and participation
    C. Adherence to organization and rationalization
    D. Emphasis on the elements of nature illuminated by science, rather than the unknown or mystical

17. Which of the following is NOT a formal perquisite granted to Congressional members?

    A. Franking privileges
    B. Discounts from Capitol shops and services
    C. Immunity from certain legal actions
    D. Allowances for travel and communication

18. Currently, _____ is known to be an element of the most effective welfare/entitlement programs in the United States.

    A. large, centrally-located offices
    B. frequent political input from politicians and community leaders
    C. an informal management style, with no rigid rules for conduct
    D. a rigidly-controlled bureaucracy, dominated by management personnel

19. The type of gene therapy that affects the subject's entire lineage from the point of intervention is

    A. mitotic intervention
    B. germ-cell therapy
    C. zygote therapy
    D. T-cell therapy

20. In general, the established evaluations of contemporary American service-industry employees (such as operators, agents, and clerks) measure the efficiency of each worker according to the

    A. speed with which each customer is handled
    B. quality of services rendered
    C. customer satisfaction
    D. profit-per-transaction

21. Which issues lies at the heart of modern Western ethics?

    A. Fate
    B. Guilt
    C. Meaninglessness
    D. Justice

22. Among typical Japanese low-wage workers, the GREATEST sense of personal shame results from

    A. failure to meet social obligations
    B. poor performance on the job
    C. low status of individual position
    D. poor living conditions

23. Which of the following is NOT generally considered to be a value or condition that would contribute to the restoration of the United States to economic vitality?

    A. Collectivism
    B. Individualism
    C. Patriotism
    D. Materialism

24. In the United States' mainstream television news broadcasts, the top stories for any given report are increasingly decided by

    A. the perceived impact of the story on the public
    B. current trends in the social and political fabric
    C. pressure from corporate sponsors
    D. the availability and interest level of video footage

25. In the developing field of human gene therapy, which is generally considered the MOST ethically unsound end for treatment?

    A. Therapeutic repair
    B. Experimental modification
    C. Composite trait selection
    D. Subjective enhancement

KEY (CORRECT ANSWERS)

1. D		26. A
2. C		27. B
3. D		28. B
4. D		29. A
5. B		30. B
6. C		31. A
7. B		32. B
8. C		33. C
9. B		34. B
10. B		35. A

21. C
22. B
23. A
24. D
25. D

TEST 4

DIRECTIONS: Each question or incomplete statement is followed by several suggested answers or completions. Select the one that BEST answers the question or completes the statement. *PRINT THE LETTER OF THE CORRECT ANSWER IN THE SPACE AT THE RIGHT.*

1. In America's formative years, which of the following was considered to be an enemy to the personal work ethic?

    A. Individualism
    B. Periods of recreation
    C. Idle time between work tasks
    D. Religious observances that interrupted work

2. Which of the following does NOT generally describe the administration of contemporary American political campaigns?

    A. Rhetorical   B. Localized
    C. Corporate   D. Mass-mediated

3. In contemporary American society, the extent of an individual's right to health care is increasingly decided by the individual's

    A. geographical proximity to the appropriate specialist
    B. severity of need
    C. awareness of the need situations
    D. ability to pay for treatment

4. Which news category has shown the GREATEST coverage increase in the last decade among mainstream news media in the United States?

    A. Politics
    B. Entertainment
    C. Social trends and problems
    D. Science and the environment

5. Since the 1920s, _____ workers have been LEAST likely to complain about the unpleasantness of working conditions in America.

    A. unskilled   B. farmers and agricultural
    C. white-collar office   D. low-level service

6. Which ethical code is based on personal duty?

    A. Deontological   B. Epistemological
    C. Teleological   D. Existential

7. The term for the element of a physician's ethical code that permits him/her to withhold information from a patient who is too frightened, unstable, or depressed to deal effectively with the information is

    A. benign malpractice   B. therapeutic privilege
    C. nonmaleficence   D. judicious restraint

13

8. Social policy in the United States, especially at the federal level, is currently thought by analysts to be oriented toward individual

   A. abilities
   B. obligations
   C. claims
   D. potentials

9. The characteristic MOST likely to restore the work ethic among industrial and service workers is

   A. obedience
   B. specialization
   C. autonomy
   D. detachment

10. Due to the nature of contemporary political campaigns, American voters are LEAST likely to receive impressions about a candidate's potential in the area of

    A. charisma
    B. issues orientation
    C. personal integrity
    D. competence

11. Each of the following is considered to be a component of America's original personal work ethic EXCEPT

    A. the gradual accumulation of material comforts
    B. a perceived moral duty to work hard
    C. pride in work skills and the quality of the resulting product or service
    D. a willingness to exert high effort to achieve material well-being

12. After their initial refusal to address the production of cheaper, better automobiles by foreign competitors, the Big Three responded by investing billions of dollars in the late 70's in

    A. robotics and machines that would eliminate paid factory positions
    B. product research and development
    C. quality-control programs
    D. personnel training and education

13. In America, the modern media GENERALLY views the consumer population as a

    A. set of differentiated groups
    B. single society
    C. confederation of individuals
    D. bureau of a few limited classes

14. Legally, a frozen human embryo's status is currently that of

    A. an individual with the right of self-determination
    B. an individual who is, until implantation, the property of an appointed legal guardian
    C. the property of the mother, who will decide its fate
    D. joint property requiring consent of both parents for development/implantation

15. Which pattern of activity was considered MOST desirable to workers in the early American agricultural society?

    A. Sustained work interrupted by brief periods of vigorous recreation
    B. Sustained work interrupted by brief periods of idle rest
    C. Intermittent periods of work with generous intervals of idle rest
    D. Sustained religious observance interrupted by brief periods of intense labor

16. The Industrial Revolution was partly responsible for the erosion of the work ethic in America because it

    A. lowered the standard of living for workers and consumers
    B. accelerated production and created more leisure time for workers
    C. reduced the workers' pride through repetitive, assembly-line tasks
    D. made managers and executives less likely to push workers to excel

17. Generally, what is the MOST influential source of values for those Americans who still practice the work ethic?

    A. Family
    B. School
    C. Work environment
    D. Religious beliefs

18. Most ethicists believe a person's ethical character to be PRIMARILY formed by

    A. societal rule and law
    B. conscious actions
    C. religious affiliation
    D. study of moral rules

19. Which of the following is NOT a category of concern currently thought to contribute to nonwork among American individuals?

    A. Economic
    B. Political
    C. Cultural
    D. Religious

20. In general, during the period from 1950-1980, how did the television entertainment industry influence the American work ethic?
    It

    A. poked fun at working-class families and lifestyles
    B. glorified the virtues of hard work
    C. avoided any reference or allusion to the middle class
    D. dealt extensively with social issues and the American workplace

21. Which word BEST describes the contemporary standards by which the population currently makes ethical assessments of public figures?

    A. Situational
    B. Traditional
    C. Absolute
    D. Relative

22. The traditional definition of equality in America includes all but _____ characteristics of the individual.

    A. rights
    B. needs
    C. obligations
    D. freedoms

23. Most ethical codes for physicians hold each of the following conditions in a patient to be signs of incompetence for informed consent EXCEPT the inability to

    A. offer a preference
    B. provide a rational reason
    C. pay for expensive, specialized services
    D. understand information

24. Which of the following topics is LEAST likely to be debated today, given the current state of American politics?

    A. Individual freedoms
    B. The extent of federal government
    C. Individual responsibilities
    D. Individual needs

25. With the use of their franking privileges, Congressional members are allowed to distribute each of the following types of postal material EXCEPT

    A. public opinion poll results
    B. biographies and pictures
    C. holiday greetings
    D. press releases that deal with legislative activity

KEY (CORRECT ANSWERS)

1. C	11. A
2. B	12. A
3. D	13. A
4. B	14. D
5. B	15. A
6. A	16. C
7. B	17. A
8. C	18. B
9. C	19. D
10. B	20. A

21. A
22. C
23. C
24. C
25. C

EXAMINATION SECTION

TEST 1

DIRECTIONS: Each question or incomplete statement is followed by several suggested answers or completions. Select the one that BEST answers the question or completes the statement. *PRINT THE LETTER OF THE CORRECT ANSWER IN THE SPACE AT THE RIGHT.*

Question 1 refers to the following passage:

Competition and the resulting race for higher productivity and new markets had costs as well as benefits. New technology demanded that factories operate at near-capacity in order to produce goods most economically. Because of this:
- The more manufacturers produced, the more they had to sell
- To sell more, they had to reduce prices
- To profit more, they expanded further and often reduced wages
- To expand, they had to borrow money
- To repay the money, they had to produce and sell even more

1. Which of the following best describes how U.S. business leaders attempted to deal with the dilemma described in the passage? 1._____
    A. They formed large enterprises that merged the assets of major competitors in an industry
    B. They developed more cooperative ways to deal with organized labor
    C. They made extensive use of the scientific management principles of Frederick Winslow Taylor
    D. They tried to increase exports by calling for the elimination of protective tariffs

2. Which of the following is the most accurate comparison of the two companies represented in the organizational charts below? 2._____

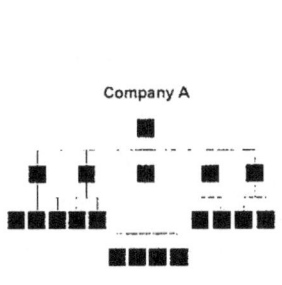
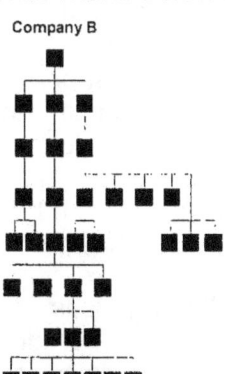

   A. The work force in Company B has considerably higher skill levels than the work force in Company A
   B. Company B is more likely than Company A to experience delays in the flow of information
   C. Lower-level managers in Company B have more decision-making authority than lower-level managers in Company A
   D. Company B is better able than Company A to adjust to unexpected changes in business conditions

3. Human resource managers can best ensure high job performance and work satisfaction among employees by
   A. basing employee compensation on current market standards
   B. putting all new employees through a comprehensive orientation process
   C. devising objective measures of employee performance
   D. developing procedures to match the right person to the right job

3._____

4. Which of the following best describes an important difference between partnerships and the corporate form of business organization?
   A. Transfer of ownership has limited effect on the status of a partnership
   B. The liability of corporate owners is limited to the amount of stock they own
   C. The life of a partnership is unlimited
   D. Corporations do not have to pay state income taxes on their profits

4._____

5. A researcher would be best advised to use a stratified sample for a marketing survey when there is a strong likelihood that
   A. factors such as age and gender will influence the answers of respondents
   B. respondents will not provide accurate answers to certain types of questions
   C. low response rates will distort the representativeness of the sample
   D. factors such as survey complexity will prevent the timely collection of data

5._____

6. Marketers should place particular emphasis on communicating the competitive advantages of a product when developing marketing strategies for which of the following types of commodities?
   A. Impulse products that consumers purchase without having planned to do so
   B. Attribute-based shopping products that consumers evaluate on the basis of product features before making a purchase
   C. Staples that are routinely purchased by consumers on a regular basis
   D. Specialty products for which consumers are willing to make special efforts to obtain preferred brands

6._____

7. Which of the following types of promotions would be the most appropriate marketing objective for a product that has entered the maturity phase of the traditional product life cycle?
   A. Informative advertising designed to increase consumer awareness of the product's attributes
   B. Motivational advertising designed to generate enthusiasm for the product
   C. Competitive advertising designed to maintain a differential advantage over competing products
   D. Persuasive advertising designed to expand market distribution of the product

7._____

8. To ensure that inventory is reordered at an appropriate time, it is most important that stores possess accurate information on which of the following?
    A. Per order processing costs and average monthly sales
    B. Total number of sales, slow-selling items and quantity discounts
    C. Order lead time, stock on hand and the usage rate
    D. Merchandise handling expenses and average inventory on hand

9. Which of the following best describes a major advantage and disadvantage of a specific advertising medium?
    A. Radio advertising enables firms to adopt a personal approach, but the per message cost is extremely high
    B. Although newspaper advertising offers a wide range of creative options, it has low credibility
    C. Direct mail advertising enables firms to target a specific audience, but there is a high throwaway rate
    D. Although magazine advertisements have a short lead time, they have low appeal to passive consumers

10. The owner of a delicatessen purchases four tables and a dozen chairs for $1,100, which will be paid in four quarterly installments during the next 12 months. Which of the following best describes the effect of this transaction on the business's accounts?
    A. Assets and owner equity increase by $1,100, and liabilities remain the same
    B. Assets, liabilities and owner equity all increase by $1,100
    C. Liabilities increase by $1,100, and assets and owner equity remain the same
    D. Both assets and liabilities increase by $1,100, and owner equity remains the same

11. Although the ToughSole Shoe Company's output and revenues have increased steadily in recent years, investors are worried about the high level of borrowing that has taken place to finance the firm's expansion. Changes in which of the following would most clearly reflect their concerns?
    A. Retained earnings
    B. Price-to-earnings ratio
    C. Dividend yield
    D. Debt-to-equity ratio

12. What amount should be recorded to retained earnings on this income statement?

12._____

```
            Worldwide Market Research, Inc.
                  Income Statement
            For month ending November 30, 20XX
         Services rendered        $11,100

    Revenues:
        Interest income              900

            Total Revenues                    $12,000

    Expenses:
        Equipment expense       $ 3,000
        Salaries expense          7,100

            Total expense                      10,100

    Net income before tax                     $ 1,900

    Provision for income tax                  $   310
```

A. $1,590
B. $2,210
C. $10,410
D. $12,310

13. Department A of Jones Retail has shown a net loss for the past two years, and company executives are thinking about eliminating the department. Based on information presented in the chart below, Jones Retail would be best advised to retain the department until its

13._____

	Avoidable Expenses	Unavoidable Expenses
Salaries of sales personnel	$ 30,000	
Advertising	3,000	
Supplies	800	
Depreciation, store equipment		$1,000
Rent		3,500
Insurance (merchandise and equipment)	1,400	400
Bad debts	400	
Share of general office expenses	600	3,800
Totals	$ 36,200	$8,700

A. unavoidable expenses exceed $36,200
B. annual loss exceeds $8,700
C. avoidable share of general office expenses exceeds $3,800
D. annual loss exceeds $36,200

14. A group discussion leader who is seeking to maximize interaction among individual group members would be best advised to adopt which of the seating arrangements shown below?

I   II   III   IV

     A. I   B. II   C. III   D. IV

15. The arithmetic, logic and control circuits are elements of which of the following parts of a computer?
    A. Main memory
    B. Central processing unit (CPU)
    C. Disk drive
    D. Disk operating system (DOS)

16. An architectural firm would most likely use computer-assisted design (CAD) software for which of the following purposes?
    A. Create a marketing plan
    B. Evaluate alternative locations for a new building
    C. Develop a prototype of a new facility
    D. Analyze the work process in the drafting room

17. In which of the following situations would satellite telecommunications best be used?
    A. Broadcasting a local radio show
    B. Conducting a class through distance learning
    C. Making an analog telephone call
    D. Conducting a job interview

18. Password security on a network can best be maintained by adopting which of the following practices?
    A. Using passwords with an odd rather than even number of letters
    B. Using passwords that use a combination of letters and numbers
    C. Assigning the same password to entire departments of a company
    D. Having users enter a different password each time they log on

19. Which of the following would most likely cause the shift shown in the supply curve?

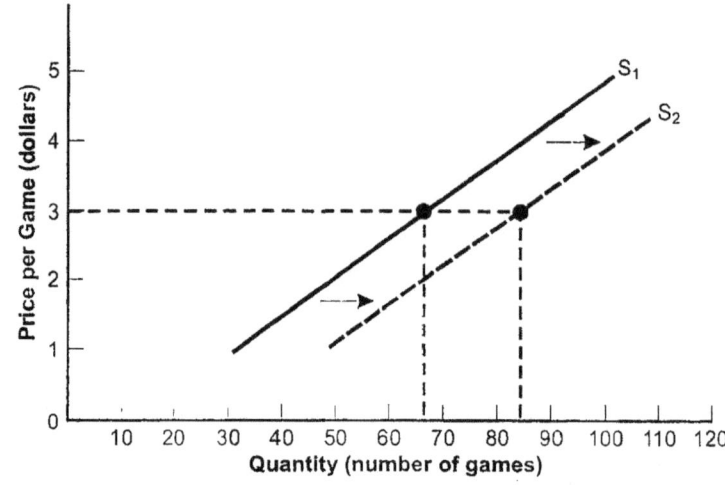

A. Introduction of more efficient ways to manufacture and distribute games
B. Increase in the labor costs of game producers
C. Development of a popular alternative form of home entertainment
D. Increase in the price of computer game players

20. Which characteristic of entrepreneurs most distinguishes them from other businesspeople?
A. Their ability to combine resources to produce goods and services
B. Their willingness to work long hours on a project
C. Their ability to develop effective operating strategies for an enterprise
D. Their willingness to take financial risks with their own capital

21. Which of the following best describes a major late-20th-century trend in international business history?
A. Major industrial powers forged expansive new free-trade pacts that hindered the economic growth of developing countries
B. Advances in communications technology created unprecedented opportunities for international trade
C. Advances in manufacturing technology forced long-time opponents of free trade to abandon protectionist practices
D. Disagreements about international labor standards prompted a resurgence of economic nationalism

22. Quality control workers at a ball-bearing plant inspect a random sample of output from company production lines each day. They are particularly concerned about any increase in the standard deviation of the bearings' diameter, as this would indicate that the
A. bearings are larger than specified
B. sample is too small for inspection purposes
C. bearings are not perfectly smooth
D. size of the bearings is inconsistent

7 (#1)

23. Susan is uncertain whether to purchase collision coverage, an optional form of auto insurance that would pay for the repair or replacement of her car if she has an accident. Susan can best decide if it is advisable to obtain the additional coverage by determining

    A. what types of damage her car is likely to sustain in various types of accidents
    B. what it would cost to replace her car, compared to the cost of the coverage
    C. what the likelihood is that she will be in an accident during the life of the policy
    D. what her car cost when it was new, compared to the cost of the coverage

23._____

Use the list below of personal attitudes and attributes to answer question 24:

- Prefers varied duties to a familiar work routine
- Performs well under pressure
- Has superior written and verbal communication skills
- Is interested in pursuing opportunities for professional development
- Enjoys working with other people
- Is able to adapt quickly to unexpected developments

24. The attitudes and attributes listed above best match the personal characteristics needed for success in which of the following business career fields?

    A. Insurance and real estate
    B. Accounting
    C. Business data processing
    D. Public relations

24._____

KEY (CORRECT ANSWERS)

1. A	11. D	21. B
2. B	12. A	22. D
3. D	13. B	23. B
4. B	14. A	24. D
5. A	15. B	
6. B	16. C	
7. C	17. B	
8. C	18. B	
9. C	19. A	
10. D	20. D	

EXAMINATION SECTION
TEST 1

DIRECTIONS: Each question or incomplete statement is followed by several suggested answers or completions. Select the one that BEST answers the question or completes the statement. *PRINT THE LETTER OF THE CORRECT ANSWER IN THE SPACE AT THE RIGHT.*

1. What type of reinforcement schedule is illustrated by a sales commission?

    A. Variable interval
    B. Variable ratio
    C. Fixed interval
    D. Fixed ratio

2. Mathematical models of management grew out of the _____ school of management.

    A. behavioral
    B. systems
    C. contingency
    D. scientific

3. *Individual equity* is the term for the extent to which

    A. pay rates allocated to specific individuals within the organization reflect variations in individual merit
    B. pay rates for particular jobs correspond to rates paid for similar jobs on the entire job market
    C. pay rates for various jobs inside the organization reflect the relative worth of those jobs
    D. compensable factors will be used to rate the worth of particular jobs

4. External audits of a company are normally performed every

    A. month
    B. quarter
    C. year
    D. two years

5. Production design is primarily concerned with _____ controls.

    A. marginal B. process C. input D. output

6. The use of profit centers is appropriate only when

    A. it is used to measure the direct profit impact of the unit's efforts
    B. the unit is responsible for revenues, but does not have control over costs of the products they handle
    C. the unit has significant control over both costs and revenues
    D. the unit has control over investment decisions

7. A human resource manager's attention should be focused *primarily* on _____ during managerial selection.

    A. job behavior
    B. education level
    C. interview results
    D. test scores

8. Which of the following computer-based information systems would be used to handle word processing?

    A. TPS B. MIS C. OAS D. DSS

9. The technique most useful for solving inventory problems is

   A. the Delphi technique
   B. EOQ
   C. queuing
   D. linear programming

10. A commission formed by a company is responsible to

    A. the general public
    B. top-level management
    C. union leaders
    D. stockholders

11. Each of the following is typically considered an ordering cost EXCEPT

    A. time
    B. paperwork
    C. pilferage
    D. postage

12. The use of scenarios may help managers to

    A. tighten day-to-day control
    B. examine different possible outcomes
    C. lengthen their reaction times
    D. anticipate the unknowable

13. During the appraisal of an employee's performance, a human resources manager tends to compare the employee with other coworkers, rather than with a performance standard. What type of rating error is occurring?

    A. Severity error
    B. Contrast error
    C. Halo effect
    D. Recency error

14. A supervisor rates a subordinate's initiative in an evaluation. This is an example of a(n) _____ measure.

    A. cognitive
    B. emotional
    C. qualitative
    D. quantitative

15. A _____ budget is NOT an operating budget.

    A. profit
    B. cash
    C. expense
    D. sales

16. Which of the following is a characteristic of a dynamic, complex company environment?

    A. Predictability
    B. Minimal need of sophisticated knowledge
    C. Numerous products and services
    D. Stability

17. A management information system is capable of each of the following EXCEPT

    A. making unprogrammed decisions
    B. providing early warning signals
    C. aiding decision-making
    D. automating clerical functions

18. In reinforcement theory, a technique that involves withholding previously available positive consequences associated with a behavior, in order to *decrease* that behavior, is known as

    A. negative reinforcement
    B. shaping
    C. punishment
    D. extinction

19. Which of the following is NOT a disadvantage associated with highly specialized, low-discretion jobs?

    A. Failing to utilize employee intelligence
    B. Can result in unproductive behaviors
    C. Requiring hiring highly trained, more expensive labor
    D. Is inconsistent with values and lifestyles of employees

20. Which of the following is an example of a line department?

    A. Production
    B. Finance
    C. Accounting
    D. Research and development

21. A computer-based OAS system is intended *primarily* to

    A. execute routine transactions
    B. allow access to historic information
    C. improve the decision-making process
    D. facilitate communication

22. The process of acquainting new employees with the policies and standards of the company is known as

    A. recruitment
    B. orientation
    C. staffing
    D. development

23. What is the term for the process of planning how to match supply with product or service demand over a time horizon of approximately one year?

    A. Capacity planning
    B. Forecasting
    C. Aggregate production planning
    D. Capacity requirements planning

24. Authority is correctly defined as the

    A. right to command and allocate resources
    B. accountability for achievement of goals and the efficient use of resources
    C. ability to influence others and control resources
    D. tendency to delegate tasks

25. According to situational leadership theory, when subordinates are able and willing to take appropriate responsibility, the appropriate leadership action is

    A. telling
    B. selling
    C. delegating
    D. participating

KEY (CORRECT ANSWERS)

1. D
2. D
3. A
4. C
5. C

6. C
7. A
8. C
9. B
10. A

11. C
12. B
13. B
14. C
15. B

16. C
17. A
18. D
19. C
20. A

21. D
22. B
23. C
24. A
25. C

TEST 2

DIRECTIONS: Each question or incomplete statement is followed by several suggested answers or completions. Select the one that BEST answers the question or completes the statement. *PRINT THE LETTER OF THE CORRECT ANSWER IN THE SPACE AT THE RIGHT.*

1. Formalized job rotation programs are an example of 1.____
   A. training
   B. career pathing
   C. recruitment
   D. career counseling

2. A(n) _____ is an example of a process layout pattern. 2.____
   A. automobile assembly line
   B. food processing plant
   C. department store
   D. hospital

3. Which of the following is MOST likely to be an output from a computerized decision support system? 3.____
   A. Projections
   B. Summary reports
   C. Special reports
   D. Schedules

4. When a company's replacement ratio is too high, 4.____
   A. replacement costs are too high
   B. there has been blocking of lower-level personnel
   C. insufficient weeding out has taken place
   D. a shortage of capable managers exists

5. An advantage associated with functional job grouping is that it 5.____
   A. facilitates organizational growth
   B. allows for easier hiring
   C. makes allocation of expenses easier
   D. facilitates coordination of top managers

6. Which of the following is an advantage associated with group decision-making? 6.____
   A. Choice of best alternative
   B. Less time-consuming
   C. Encouragement of innovative thinking
   D. Lower cost

7. On an organization chart, a solid line represents a(n) 7.____
   A. vertically integrated distribution channel
   B. indirect authority relationship
   C. horizontally integrated distribution channel
   D. line authority relationship

8. Which type of power, if exercised by a manager, is most likely to secure the commitment of subordinates? 8.____
   A. Legitimate
   B. Reward
   C. Information
   D. Referent

9. Which functional area of a company involves employee relations?

   A. Finance
   B. Marketing
   C. Operations
   D. Development

10. In a restaurant, a manager tallies the number of meals that are served within 15 minutes of the customer orders. Which type of statistical quality control measure is the manager using?

    A. Input   B. Marginal   C. Attribute   D. Variable

11. Low-level analysis is most likely to be processed by which of the following kinds of computer information systems?

    A. TPS   B. DSS   C. OAS   D. MIS

12. Of the following, bottom-up budgeting best incorporates

    A. information on markets
    B. company planning parameters
    C. corporate goals
    D. industry projections

13. A worker experiences role _____ when his/her role within the organization is unclear.

    A. discord
    B. confusion
    C. ambiguity
    D. conflict

14. Which of the following is a DISADVANTAGE associated with the use of pay as an enforcer of employee performance?

    A. Time lag
    B. Low employee value
    C. Unequal pay among employees
    D. Erosion of value due to inflation

15. A company forms a temporary task force to study a problem in the community, and the company's relationship to that problem. In terms of forming responses to social issues, the company is practicing

    A. implicit change
    B. structural change
    C. tokenism
    D. functional change

16. A manager cannot assign probabilities to outcomes because he lacks information. The manager is said to be making a decision under the condition of

    A. peril
    B. certainty
    C. uncertainty
    D. risk

17. Using the resource dependence approach to controls, a manager determines that her unit is highly dependent on another unit for a particular resource, and that the expected resource flows are unacceptable. It is also determined, however, that the control process is probably not feasible for her department.
The manager should

    A. do nothing
    B. research a way to lower costs
    C. develop alternatives to control
    D. initiate the control process and try to adjust as it progresses

18. In the path–goal theory of leadership, the monitoring and control aspects of a leader's behavior are examples of _____ behavior.

    A. participative   B. supportive
    C. instrumental   D. goal–oriented

19. When a particular task is simple and morale is not an issue, _____ communication is probably the best method.

    A. circle   B. chain
    C. wheel   D. all–channel

20. In production and operations control, establishing a wage and salary structure is a function of

    A. production planning   B. production design
    C. production evaluation D. selection

21. Which of the following is a type of inventory that consists of raw materials, components, and subassemblies that are used in the production of an end product or service?

    A. Dependent demand inventory
    B. Bill of materials
    C. Independent demand inventory
    D. Cost inventory

22. _____ job testing is a means of measuring mainly mental, mechanical, and clerical capacities.

    A. Personality   B. Ability
    C. Performance   D. Replacement

23. Historically, the management theory that first emphasized the need for companies to operate in a rational manner rather than according to the whims of owners and managers was the theory of _____ management.

    A. behaviorist   B. quantitative
    C. administrative   D. bureaucratic

24. Which of the following is an example of *discretionary* costs?

    A. Raw materials   B. Mortgages
    C. Sales commissions   D. Accounting fees

25. According to the systems approach to management, a system that operates in continual interaction with its environment is a(n) _____ system.
   A. open	B. feedback	C. charged	D. looped

KEY (CORRECT ANSWERS)

1. A	11. D
2. C	12. A
3. C	13. C
4. B	14. A
5. B	15. D
6. A	16. C
7. D	17. C
8. D	18. C
9. C	19. C
10. C	20. B

21. A
22. B
23. D
24. D
25. A

TEST 3

DIRECTIONS: Each question or incomplete statement is followed by several suggested answers or completions. Select the one that BEST answers the question or completes the statement. *PRINT THE LETTER OF THE CORRECT ANSWER IN THE SPACE AT THE RIGHT.*

1. In a complex organization, the process of differentiation is likely to create problems associated with

    A. controlling size
    B. management training
    C. coordination
    D. motivation

2. Before a company can determine whether a management information system can be developed, a(n) _____ must be performed.

    A. algorithm
    B. organizational chart
    C. feasibility study
    D. conversion

3. Job testing is considered to be reliable when

    A. a good test score is a clear predictor of job success
    B. the test measures what it professes to measure
    C. the test is clearly related to the job
    D. the candidate would earn roughly the same score if the test were repeated

4. A control system that is self-regulating is said to be

    A. formalized
    B. feedback-looped
    C. cybernetic
    D. centralized

5. A company with many rules and procedures is usually described as having a(n) _____ span of control.

    A. almost nonexistent
    B. narrow
    C. moderate
    D. wide

6. Altogether, the various types of financial statements are considered _____ control.

    A. input   B. output   C. process   D. steering

7. A human resources manager teaches a new employee what to do, where to go for help, and what the company's important rules and policies are. What stage of orientation is being transacted?

    A. Implementation
    B. Socialization
    C. Induction
    D. Evaluation

8. The factors necessary in order to estimate partial-factor productivity are _____ and goods/services produced.

    A. labor hours
    B. labor hours, capital,
    C. capital, energy, materials,
    D. labor hours, capital, energy, technology, materials,

9. A company's _____ policy will decide the channels of distribution for a given product.

    A. financial
    B. personnel
    C. marketing
    D. product

10. Which of the following factors favors decentralization of computerized information system resources?

    A. Increasing availability of user–friendly software
    B. Staff specialization
    C. Easier control of corporate databases
    D. Potential for economies of scale

11. Each of the following typically helps implement authority in an organization EXCEPT

    A. span of control
    B. centralization
    C. chain of command
    D. familiarity

12. A maintenance goal

    A. implies a specific level of activity over time
    B. expresses the hope for growth
    C. uses action verbs to indicate change
    D. implies an effort to reorganize

13. Each of the following is a potential pitfall associated with financial controls EXCEPT

    A. neglecting to link controls to strategic planning process
    B. stifling innovation and creativity
    C. not sophisticated enough for organizational needs
    D. mixed messages about desired behaviors

14. The term for a statement of the skills, abilities, education, and previous work experience required to perform a particular job is the

    A. replacement chart
    B. job specification
    C. job description
    D. job analysis

15. The most successful use of the practice of job rotation is

    A. to create maximum flexibility through cross–training
    B. as an employee development tool
    C. to alleviate boredom with simple jobs
    D. to improve departmental loyalty

16. A company vice president delegates the authority to make a decision to a product manager. This is an example of

    A. outsourcing
    B. horizontal decentralization
    C. vertical decentralization
    D. centralized decision–making

17. Time–and–motion studies were first carried out by the _____ school of management.

    A. scientific
    B. human relations
    C. classical
    D. contingency

18. What is the term for the dispersion of organizational power?

    A. Unity of command
    B. Span of control
    C. Formalization
    D. Decentralization

19. _____ is the term for a technique to enhance creativity that relies on analogies.

    A. Storming
    B. Entropy
    C. Cybernetics
    D. Synectics

20. Which of the following is NOT considered to be a limitation associated with organization charts?

    A. May not indicate real power and influence of people on the chart
    B. Does not show a picture of the structure at a particular point in time
    C. Frequently outdated
    D. May not show actual formal relationships

21. Which of the following is considered to be a *snapshot* of an organization at a particular point in time?

    A. Expense budget
    B. Income statement
    C. Balance sheet
    D. Cash flow statement

22. Each of the following would be considered a safety and security need for an employee EXCEPT

    A. merit pay raises
    B. job security
    C. pay raises references to the cost of living
    D. benefits

23. The behavioral model of management contributed the idea of

    A. quantitative aids for decision-making
    B. organization members as active human resources
    C. the potential importance of the environment to organizational success
    D. the need for a scientific approach to management

24. According to the contingency perspective, which of the following would NOT be a major contingency factor for a business?

    A. Strategy
    B. Size
    C. External environment
    D. Technology in use

25. Which of the following is NOT an example of a single-use plan?

    A. Standing plan
    B. Budget
    C. Project
    D. Program

KEY (CORRECT ANSWERS)

1. B
2. C
3. D
4. C
5. D

6. B
7. C
8. A
9. C
10. A

11. D
12. A
13. C
14. B
15. B

16. C
17. C
18. D
19. D
20. B

21. C
22. A
23. B
24. B
25. A

EXAMINATION SECTION
TEST 1

DIRECTIONS: Each question or incomplete statement is followed by several suggested answers or completions. Select the one that BEST answers the question or completes the statement. *PRINT THE LETTER OF THE CORRECT ANSWER IN THE SPACE AT THE RIGHT.*

1. In production and operations control, choosing the site of the production facility is a function of the _____ process. 1._____

    A. production design
    B. selection
    C. production planning
    D. production evaluation

2. Each of the following is an advantage associated with high job specialization EXCEPT for 2._____

    A. facilitating scientific method study
    B. saving time in switching from one task to another
    C. being well-suited to small, entrepreneurial companies
    D. increasing worker dexterity

3. A statement of the duties, working conditions, and other significant requirements associated with a particular job is termed a 3._____

    A. replacement chart
    B. job specification
    C. job description
    D. job analysis

4. A _____ organizational plan is illustrated by a company's method for figuring overtime pay. 4._____

    A. short-term
    B. long-term
    C. single-use
    D. standing

5. Which of the following files lists the names and quantities of all items that are required to produce one unit of product? 5._____

    A. Inventory
    B. Output
    C. MRP
    D. Bill of materials

6. Which of the following is NOT a branch of the quantitative management approach? 6._____

    A. Behavioral science
    B. Management information systems
    C. Operations management
    D. Management science

7. During a staff development meeting, several employees are asked to view some videotapes that illustrate a process related to job performance, and are then asked to tape and observe their own performance of this activity.
This is an example of 7._____

    A. understudy
    B. socialization
    C. behavior modeling
    D. apprenticeship

8. _____ is a statistical technique that involves evaluating random samples from a group of produced materials to determine whether the group meets agreeable quality levels.

   A. Statistical process control
   B. Acceptance sampling
   C. Raw materials sampling
   D. AQL

8._____

9. A formal business group, consisting of a manager and all the subordinates who report to that manager, is known as a(n)

   A. strategic business unit   B. reference group
   C. command group   D. module

9._____

10. Which of the following ideas was contributed by the classical viewpoint of management?

    A. The visualization of organizations as systems of interrelated parts
    B. The managerial importance of leadership
    C. There is no one best way to manage
    D. The importance of pay as a motivator

10._____

11. Each of the following is a component of quality control EXCEPT

    A. marketability   B. function
    C. aesthetics   D. safety

11._____

12. The human resource needs of a company are determined *primarily* by

    A. a human resource audit
    B. the company's goals and strategies
    C. the legal environment
    D. a replacement chart

12._____

13. If an employee is terminated as a result of _____, this is an example of *due cause*.

    A. layoff   B. incompetence
    C. retirement   D. plant closing

13._____

14. According to the systems approach to management, there are four major components to an organizational system. Which of the following is NOT one of these components?

    A. Inputs   B. Transformation processes
    C. Feedback   D. Raw materials

14._____

15. Tactical problems are *primarily* the responsibility of

    A. workers   B. low–level managers
    C. middle–level managers   D. executives

15._____

16. Robert Owens' (1771–1858) contribution to management theory involved

    A. human resources   B. cognitive theory
    C. work specialization   D. behaviorist theory

16._____

17. The _____ dimension of quality involves the degree to which a product's design or operating characteristics meet established standards.

    A. reliability
    B. conformance
    C. serviceability
    D. durability

18. Which type of technology is illustrated by a commercial bank?

    A. Long–linked
    B. Intensive
    C. Long–term
    D. Mediating

19. According to situational leadership theory, the technique of *telling* is used when followers are

    A. able to take responsibility but are unwilling or too insecure to do so
    B. able and willing to take responsibility
    C. unable to take responsibility but are willing to do so
    D. unable and unwilling or too insecure to take responsibility for a given task

20. The principles of management by objectives (MBO) include each of the following EXCEPT

    A. executive–proposed goals
    B. managerial–subordinate discussion
    C. mutual goal–setting
    D. performance feedback

21. Each of the following is considered to be a valuable characteristic of layout design EXCEPT

    A. reduction of material transport cost, but not time
    B. bottleneck–free floor design
    C. employee safety provisions
    D. minimizing travel distance required for worker to reach materials

22. What stage of group development deals with accomplishing assigned tasks?

    A. Internal problem–solving
    B. Growth and productivity
    C. Orientation
    D. Evaluation and control

23. Typically, which of the following steps in the budgetary process would occur FIRST?

    A. Unit manager formulation of unit's operating plans
    B. Top management outlines resource restraints
    C. Top management combines information
    D. Unit managers determine resource needs

24. In a matching analysis, what has occurred when an external opportunity matches the internal strength of a company?

    A. Problem
    B. Vulnerability
    C. Leverage
    D. Constraint

24.____

25. What type of reinforcement schedule is illustrated by a weekly paycheck?

    A. Variable interval
    B. Variable ratio
    C. Fixed interval
    D. Fixed ratio

25.____

KEY (CORRECT ANSWERS)

1.	B	11.	A
2.	C	12.	B
3.	C	13.	B
4.	D	14.	D
5.	D	15.	C
6.	A	16.	A
7.	C	17.	B
8.	B	18.	D
9.	C	19.	D
10.	D	20.	A

21. A
22. B
23. B
24. C
25. C

TEST 2

DIRECTIONS: Each question or incomplete statement is followed by several suggested answers or completions. Select the one that BEST answers the question or completes the statement. *PRINT THE LETTER OF THE CORRECT ANSWER IN THE SPACE AT THE RIGHT.*

1. A management approach that is oblivious to ethical considerations is described as   1._____

   A. unethical   B. amoral   C. libertine   D. immoral

2. Informal leaders could serve a valuable role in a company when   2._____

   A. they defer to organizational power
   B. their influence is compatible with the company's goals
   C. they make other people feel satisfied with their own performance
   D. their activity receives praise from higher management

3. Moving from marketing to production is an example of a(n) _____ of career path.   3._____

   A. vertical   B. circumferential
   C. radial   D. cone

4. Each of the following is a DISADVANTAGE associated with the use of a rational model for decision–making in a company EXCEPT   4._____

   A. preferences cannot be ranked in a permanent way
   B. payoffs are difficult to estimate
   C. not all necessary information is available
   D. environmental conditions cannot be accurately forecast

5. The MAIN advantage to product departmentalization is   5._____

   A. duplication of efforts
   B. adaptability
   C. achieving economies of scale
   D. innovation

6. The decision to hire a new employee is a(n) _____ decision.   6._____

   A. programmed   B. nonprogrammed
   C. detail   D. under certainty

7. Which of the following are concerned with departmental or interdepartmental activities?   7._____

   A. Policies   B. Procedures
   C. Rules   D. Goals and strategies

8. Each of the following is a legal concern associated with job testing EXCEPT   8._____

   A. length of the test
   B. reliability of the test
   C. relation of test to the job
   D. whether test measures what it professes to measure

9. The settling of disputes over contract language during collective bargaining is known as _____ arbitration.   9._____

   A. interest   B. verbal   C. rights   D. contract

41

10. In an oligopolistic economic environment, there are _____ sellers and _____ buyers.

    A. many; few
    B. many; many
    C. few; many
    D. few; few

11. What term would be used to describe a company whose decision-making power is dispersed among lower-level managers?

    A. Thin
    B. Decentralized
    C. Flat
    D. Fat

12. The effort to solve problems by beginning with a problem and attempting to move logically to a solution is known as

    A. the rational model
    B. convergent thinking
    C. the incremental model
    D. divergent thinking

13. If a manager determines that controls are needed but the control process will be too costly, each of the following is an alternative to controls EXCEPT

    A. changing the dependence relationship
    B. implementing horizontal integration
    C. changing organizational goals and objectives to eliminate dependence
    D. changing the nature of the dependence

14. Each of the following is an advantage associated with the use of internal recruitment in the management of human resources EXCEPT

    A. availability of reliable candidate information
    B. rewarding of good performance
    C. increased internal morale due to upward mobility opportunities
    D. increased likelihood of new ideas being introduced

15. A company uses an organizational design in which a product structure overlays a functional structure. What type of design structure is being used?

    A. Functional
    B. Matrix
    C. Contingency
    D. Classical

16. The allocation of a company's financial resources is known as the _____ process.

    A. capital development
    B. financial evaluation
    C. budgeting
    D. equity sourcing

17. Developing plans, setting goals, and making decisions are part of

    A. coordination
    B. influencing
    C. formulation
    D. implementation

18. Generally, the consumerism movement is concerned with each of the following EXCEPT

    A. price fixing
    B. retail complaint-handling
    C. equal opportunity employment
    D. deceptive labeling

19. A company's management sets a goal of achieving a 12% return on investment capital from the sale of a company's product line. What type of goal has the company set?

   A. Operative
   B. Official
   C. Operational
   D. Short-term

20. When a company's turnover rate is too low,

   A. replacement costs are too high
   B. there has been blocking of lower-level personnel
   C. insufficient weeding out has taken place
   D. a shortage of capable managers exists

21. A ratio that compares the owner's financial contributions to a company with creditors' contributions is called the _____ ratio.

   A. leverage
   B. profitability
   C. liquidity
   D. operating

22. The production evaluation process is primarily concerned with _____ control.

   A. input
   B. output
   C. marginal
   D. process

23. _____ is considered a structural barrier to managerial automation.

   A. Incompatible systems
   B. Uncertainty avoidance
   C. Resistance
   D. A reward system that emphasizes quick and dramatic results

24. After an affirmative action plan has been written by a reporting company, a copy is required to be forwarded to the

   A. Department of Labor
   B. Equal Employment Opportunity Commission (EEOC)
   C. National Labor Relations Board
   D. Department of Human Service

25. Historically, the management theory that first focused on principles that could be used by managers to coordinate the internal activities of organizations was the theory of _____ management.

   A. behaviorist
   B. quantitative
   C. administrative
   D. bureaucratic

KEY (CORRECT ANSWERS)

1.	B	11.	B
2.	B	12.	B
3.	B	13.	B
4.	C	14.	D
5.	B	15.	B
6.	A	16.	C
7.	B	17.	C
8.	A	18.	C
9.	A	19.	A
10.	C	20.	C

21. A
22. B
23. D
24. A
25. C

TEST 3

DIRECTIONS: Each question or incomplete statement is followed by several suggested answers or completions. Select the one that BEST answers the question or completes the statement. *PRINT THE LETTER OF THE CORRECT ANSWER IN THE SPACE AT THE RIGHT.*

1. Which of the following is a financial resource for a company?

    A. Raw material reserves
    B. Reputation for quality
    C. Bond issues
    D. Warehouses

2. Discretionary expense centers are LEAST likely to be used with _____ departments.

    A. finance
    B. human resources
    C. research and development
    D. public relations

3. _____ managerial power is said to come from the individual, rather than from the company.

    A. Coercive
    B. Reward
    C. Expert
    D. Legitimate

4. The data inputs to computer-based executive support-systems are probably

    A. transactions
    B. aggregate data
    C. high-volume data
    D. analytic models

5. What type of audit involves the evaluation and assessment of an entire company's operations?

    A. Management
    B. Social
    C. External
    D. Internal

6. Performance feedback that is NOT evaluative is described as

    A. informal
    B. reinforcing
    C. dispersed
    D. informational

7. Which type of leader power stems from a position's placement in the managerial hierarchy and the authority vested in the position?

    A. Legitimate
    B. Referent
    C. Expert
    D. Reward

8. In matrix organizations, the BEST strategy for conflict resolution is typically

    A. conciliation
    B. consensus
    C. confrontation
    D. aversion

9. Which of the following is a destructive force that is MOST likely to affect the implementation phase of the development of a quality circle?

    A. Disagreement on problems
    B. Raised aspirations
    C. Prohibitive costs
    D. Burnout

10. An accountant who audits a company's books would use the _____ style of decision-making.

    A. intuitive B. systematic
    C. compensatory D. preceptive

11. Which functional area of a company involves equity ratio?

    A. Finance B. Marketing
    C. Operations D. Development

12. A company's plan for the acquisition or divestiture of major fixed assets is the

    A. profit budget
    B. balance sheet
    C. expense budget
    D. capital expenditures budget

13. The main DISADVANTAGE associated with job simplification is

    A. higher training costs
    B. lack of quality control mechanism
    C. lowered employee motivation
    D. loss of production efficiency

14. A company uses a compensation system in which employees throughout the organization are encouraged to become involved in solving problems, and are given bonuses tied to organizational performance improvements.
    This is an example of

    A. skill-based pay B. gainsharing
    C. benchmarking D. expanded commission

15. A task force formed by a company is responsible to

    A. the local community B. top-level management
    C. union leaders D. stockholders

16. What is the term for the identification of a trend and smoothing its pattern?

    A. Segmentation B. Moving average
    C. Time-series analysis D. Replacement analysis

17. _____ is a term for grouping jobs horizontally.

    A. Aggregation B. Departmentalization
    C. Formalization D. Dispersion

18. Which type of power, if exercised by a manager, is MOST likely to result in resistance by subordinates?

    A. Reward B. Expert C. Coercive D. Referent

19. In manufacturing, MRP systems use three major inputs. Which of the following is NOT one of these three? 19._____

   A. Bill of materials information
   B. Investment information
   C. Inventory status information
   D. Master production schedule

20. What type of quality control is concerned *primarily* with the quality of raw input materials? 20._____

   A. Output
   B. Feed–forward
   C. Feedback
   D. Work in process

21. When groups are slow to reach a decision, they are demonstrating 21._____

   A. assembly effect
   B. entropy
   C. process loss
   D. synergy

22. _____ costs are those associated with acquiring raw materials. 22._____

   A. Storage
   B. Contingency
   C. Order
   D. Carrying

23. An effective managerial control system is each of the following EXCEPT 23._____

   A. focused
   B. flexible
   C. future–oriented
   D. timely

24. During what stage of orientation does an employee acquire technical skills that are likely to improve her current job performance? 24._____

   A. Induction
   B. Implementation
   C. Socialization
   D. Training

25. In a bureaucracy, the practice of adding unnecessary subordinates is likely to create 25._____

   A. red tape
   B. position protection
   C. dominance of authority
   D. inflexibility

KEY (CORRECT ANSWERS)

1. C
2. A
3. C
4. B
5. A

6. D
7. A
8. C
9. C
10. B

11. A
12. D
13. C
14. B
15. B

16. C
17. B
18. C
19. B
20. B

21. C
22. C
23. A
24. D
25. C

EXAMINATION SECTION
TEST 1

DIRECTIONS: Each question or incomplete statement is followed by several suggested answers or completions. Select the one that BEST answers the question or completes the statement. *PRINT THE LETTER OF THE CORRECT ANSWER IN THE SPACE AT THE RIGHT.*

1. An advantage of forming a business plan is that it   1.____
   A. is a necessary part of *going public*
   B. ensures that no one steals your business idea
   C. is helpful in order to obtain outside financing
   D. protects against unlimited liability

2. A distribution system in which all retail-level marketing functions are managed by producers is called a(n) _____ distribution system.   2.____
   A. corporate   B. channel of
   C. contractual   D. administered

3. The study of the behavior of people in specific markets is called   3.____
   A. macroeconomics   B. microeconomics
   C. market segmentation   D. market targeting

4. Compensation based on an employee's acquisition of new skills is termed   4.____
   A. profit-sharing   B. goal-sharing
   C. knowledge-based pay   D. pay for performance

5. An organization owned by members who pay an annual membership fee and share in any profits is a(n)   5.____
   A. partnership   B. cooperative
   C. S corporation   D. limited partnership

6. The total output of goods and services divided by work hours equals   6.____
   A. profit   B. trial balance
   C. assets   D. productivity

7. If a company needs to adjust to a shrinking business, but wants to avoid massive layoffs, it should   7.____
   A. restructure   B. terminate
   C. outplace   D. downsize

8. Which term refers to innovative, entrepreneurial units operating on the margins of a corporation?   8.____
   A. Truck jobber   B. Rack jobber
   C. Skunkworks   D. Piggyback

9. One of the basic assumptions of Management Theory Y is that the average person   9.____
   A. wants security above all else
   B. feels that work is as natural as rest or play

49

C. wishes to be directed
D. dislikes work

10. The right to use a business's name and sell its products in a given area is called a

    A. franchise
    B. franchise agreement
    C. target market
    D. marketing mix

11. Which of the following techniques is used to control inventory?

    A. Hard manufacturing
    B. Repetitive manufacturing
    C. Material requirements planning
    D. Flexible manufacturing

12. An entity which resembles a corporation, but which is taxed like a partnership, is called a(n)

    A. limited partnership
    B. small business
    C. savings and loan
    D. S corporation

13. The study and use of ergonomics is an example of

    A. methods improvement
    B. the just-in-time system
    C. material requirements planning
    D. quality assurance

14. An agreement which allows employers to hire anyone, but which employees must pay union fees even though they do not have the right to join unions, is called a(n) _____ agreement.

    A. closed-shop
    B. agency shop
    C. collective bargaining
    D. franchise

15. An example of a consumer market is a

    A. copy machine company who sells machines to corporations
    B. clothing company who sells to department stores
    C. furniture company which specializes in office furniture for businesses
    D. furniture store which specializes in home office and conventional furniture

16. The idea that a country should produce and sell to other countries those products that it produces most efficiently is called

    A. comparative advantage
    B. absolute advantage
    C. extrinsic reward
    D. competition-oriented pricing

17. The rise of fast-food restaurants devoted to healthier eating is an example of a company responding to which aspect of the external environment?

    A. Competition
    B. Economic forces
    C. Technology
    D. Social trends

18. Wrongful conduct which results in injury to another person's body, property or reputation is called

    A. tort
    B. strict liability
    C. rule of indemnity
    D. statutory grievance

19. The influence of family members, friends, and colleagues are examples of which aspect of buyer behavior?

    A. Situational factors
    B. Reference groups
    C. Culture
    D. Social class

20. Utilizing a high-quality image in order to convey status, increase desirability, and charge more for a product is part of which aspect of the marketing mix?

    A. Product
    B. Place
    C. Price
    D. Promotion

21. A person with entrepreneurial skills who works in a corporation to launch new products is called a(n)

    A. corporate entrepreneur
    B. start-up
    C. entrepreneurial manager
    D. intrapreneur

22. Targeting consumers in Hawaii and Florida as potential purchasers of a new suntan lotion is an example of which type of market segmentation?

    A. Psychographic
    B. Behavioral
    C. Geographic
    D. Demographic

23. A _____ provides the issuer of a bond the right to retire the bond before it matures.

    A. call provision
    B. closed-shop agreement
    C. convertible bond
    D. debenture bond

24. A demand deposit is an example of

    A. plastic money
    B. a time deposit
    C. M1
    D. M2

25. Using accounts receivable as security is called

    A. hedging
    B. pledging
    C. inventory financing
    D. factoring

KEY (CORRECT ANSWERS)

1. C
2. D
3. B
4. C
5. B

6. D
7. A
8. C
9. B
10. A

11. C
12. D
13. A
14. B
15. D

16. A
17. D
18. A
19. B
20. C

21. D
22. C
23. A
24. C
25. B

TEST 2

DIRECTIONS: Each question or incomplete statement is followed by several suggested answers or completions. Select the one that BEST answers the question or completes the statement. *PRINT THE LETTER OF THE CORRECT ANSWER IN THE SPACE AT THE RIGHT.*

1. The business to whom a check is written is the

   A. time depositor
   B. demand depositor
   C. payor
   D. payee

2. Net sales minus the cost of goods sold equals the

   A. income statement
   B. gross margin
   C. balance of payments
   D. gross national product

3. A nonprofit member-owned cooperative offering checking and savings accounts and consumer loans is called a

   A. credit union
   B. savings and loan
   C. savings bank
   D. state bank

4. When a person buys stocks by borrowing some of the purchase cost from the broker, they are

   A. diversifying
   B. dumping
   C. buying on margin
   D. countertrading

5. A series of points on a graph which shows the relationship between price and quantity supplied is the

   A. demand
   B. equilibrium price
   C. demand curve
   D. supply curve

6. Buying and selling in the futures market equal and opposite to what the buyer currently has is called

   A. factoring
   B. pledging
   C. hedging
   D. speculating

7. Which of the following measures can a country take to protect its industries from importers?

   A. Tariffs
   B. Boycotts
   C. Absolute advantage measures
   D. Comparative advantage measures

8. Which of the following is likely to produce pressures causing management practices to become more innovative?

   A. Elimination of trading blocs
   B. Demographic shifts
   C. Increases in the GNP
   D. Depression or recession

9. Which pricing method assigns high prices to products in order to make optimum profit while there is little or no competition?

   A. Competition-oriented pricing
   B. Demand-oriented pricing
   C. Exclusive distribution
   D. Skimming price strategy

10. The Gross Domestic Product includes the _____ goods and services produced by the economy.

    A. dollar value of all
    B. total value of all reported and unreported
    C. dollar value of all reported and unreported
    D. total value of all

11. Which form of business ownership is the easiest and least expensive to start?

    A. Franchise
    B. Partnership
    C. Sole proprietorship
    D. Corporation

12. The pricing strategy based on consumer demand is called

    A. competition-oriented pricing
    B. demand-oriented pricing
    C. demand-pull inflation
    D. cost-push inflation

13. Which of the following are forms of partnership?
    I. General
    II. Limited
    III. Corporate
    IV. Master limited

    The CORRECT answer is:
    A. I, II, IV
    B. I, II, III
    C. II, III, IV
    D. I, II, III, IV

14. Which of the following are common categories for financing a small business?
    I. Venture capitalists
    II. Debt financing
    III. Public stock offerings
    IV. Equity financing

    The CORRECT answer is:
    A. I, II
    B. II, IV
    C. I, II, III
    D. I, II, III, IV

15. When manufacturers advertise to wholesalers and retailers, it is called

    A. internal marketing
    B. test marketing
    C. trade advertising
    D. subfranchise marketing

16. Deciding to buy a book because of its placement in a prominent place in the bookstore is an example of which aspect of buyer behavior?   16.____

    A. Culture
    B. Situational factor
    C. Social class
    D. Self-image

17. When two firms join in the same industry, it is called a   17.____

    A. merger
    B. hostile takeover
    C. vertical merger
    D. horizontal merger

18. Personal computers are examples of   18.____

    A. workstations
    B. mainframe computers
    C. microcomputers
    D. minicomputers

19. The most basic form of ownership of firms is called _____ stock.   19.____

    A. common   B. blue-chip   C. income   D. preferred

20. Computer systems which are required to process new information instantly use _____ processing.   20.____

    A. micro   B. real-time   C. batch   D. parallel

21. A computer system which imitates the thought processes of a human expert in a particular field is using   21.____

    A. a microprocessor
    B. a language processor
    C. artificial intelligence
    D. an expert system

22. Employment activities which give preference to females and minorities in an attempt to *right past wrongs* is called   22.____

    A. affirmative action
    B. fringe benefits
    C. right-to-work laws
    D. public relations

23. Which of the following are among the index of leading economic indicators?   23.____
    I. Stock market
    II. Housing starts
    III. Length of workweek
    IV. Consumer confidence

    The CORRECT answer is:
    A. I, II
    B. I, II, IV
    C. II, III, IV
    D. I, II, III, IV

24. The records system which allows information from accounting journals to be categorized so that managers can find all the information about a single account in one place is a   24.____

    A. balance sheet
    B. ledger
    C. business plan
    D. budget sheet

25. Country A exported $2 million of goods in 1998, and imported $1 million. The $1 million difference is known as the

    A. balance of payments
    B. trade deficit
    C. balance of trade
    D. trade surplus

KEY (CORRECT ANSWERS)

1.	D	11.	C
2.	B	12.	B
3.	A	13.	A
4.	C	14.	B
5.	D	15.	C
6.	C	16.	B
7.	A	17.	D
8.	B	18.	C
9.	D	19.	A
10.	A	20.	B

21.	D
22.	A
23.	B
24.	B
25.	D

EXAMINATION SECTION
TEST 1

DIRECTIONS: Each question or incomplete statement is followed by several suggested answers or completions. Select the one that BEST answers the question or completes the statement. *PRINT THE LETTER OF THE CORRECT ANSWER IN THE SPACE AT THE RIGHT.*

1. Willful violations of OSHA provisions by a corporate employer are punishable by maximum fines of up to _____ upon criminal conviction.

    A. $5,000   B. $50,000   C. $250,000   D. $500,000

2. Which of the following occurs when employees perceive too narrow a difference between their own pay and that of other colleagues?

    A. Pay compression
    B. Wage inflation
    C. Pay survey
    D. Skills gap

3. A local union typically engages in each of the following activities EXCEPT

    A. administering contracts
    B. training union leaders
    C. organizing campaigns
    D. collecting dues

4. Under existing laws or mandates, affirmative action programs are mandated for the hiring practices of

    A. public educational institutions
    B. government contractors
    C. federal agencies
    D. all of the above

5. In evaluating a training program, a human resources professional wants specifically to learn whether the knowledge, skills, or abilities learned in training led to an employee's improved performance on the job. Her evaluation of the program would test for _____ validity.

    A. training
    B. transfer
    C. intraorganizational
    D. interorganizational

6. In human resources, *methods study* is concerned with

    A. the way in which work is distributed among personnel
    B. determining the most efficient way of doing a task or job
    C. determining the minimum number of employees needed to complete a task or job
    D. the criteria used to hire employees

7. Which of the following is/are advantages associated with internal recruiting?
    I. It offers loyal employees a fair chance at promotion.
    II. It helps protect trade secrets.
    III. It encourages new ideas and competition.

    The CORRECT answer is:

    A. I only   B. III only   C. I, II   D. II, III

8. In the vocabulary of job analysis, coordinated and aggregated series of work elements that are used to produce a specific output are referred to as

   A. positions   B. jobs   C. chores   D. tasks

9. During the personnel selection process, human resource professionals sometimes use selection tests that are designed to have what is called *predictive validity*. The primary drawback to using this type of assessment is that

   A. employees are often unwilling to take extensive test batteries
   B. an employer must wait until a large enough *predictive* group has been hired to norm the measurement
   C. *self-selection* bias can restrict the range of test scores
   D. results are often skewed toward applicants with previous experience

10. Jobs whose salaries are below the minimum of the salary range for the job are described as _____ jobs.

    A. broadband   B. red circle
    C. green circle   D. exempt

11. In an organization with a human resources department, which of the following information is most likely to be covered by the operating supervisor in orienting a new employee?

    A. A brief history of the organization
    B. Rules, regulations, policies, and procedures
    C. Personnel policies
    D. Reviewing performance criteria

12. In human resources management, *pay structure* refers to

    A. pay set relative to employees working on different jobs within the organization
    B. a grouping of a variety of work jobs that are similar in their difficulty and responsibility requirements
    C. pay set relative to employees working on similar jobs in other organizations
    D. a survey of the compensation of all employees by all employers in a geographic area, an industry, or an occupational group

13. Which of the following is a provision of the Rehabilitation Act, as amended?

    A. Employers may not cite the potential legal liability for drug-related injuries or accidents as a reason for firing an employee.
    B. Employers of 100 or more must establish employee assistance programs (EAPs) for helping drug addicts or alcoholics to recover.
    C. Employers of any size may not fire, or refuse to hire, an employee or candidate solely because of alcohol or drug addiction.
    D. Drug addiction and alcoholism are not be be considered *disabilities* in the same category as other employee handicaps.

14. A disadvantage of using ranking as a job evaluation method is that

    A. it is the slowest of all job evaluation methods
    B. it requires cumbersome descriptions of each job class
    C. it is one of the more expensive methods
    D. its results are nearly always more subjective than with other methods

15. In an organization that employs at least some union members, union members are sometimes given preferences over nonunion members in areas such as hiring, promotion, and layoff. Preferences given in this situation are often likely to violate the provisions of the _____ Act.

    A. Taft-Hartley
    B. Wagner
    C. Landrum-Griffin
    D. Fair Labor Standards

16. In human resources management, the _____ principle states that authority flows one link at a time, from the top of the organization to the bottom.

    A. parity
    B. scalar
    C. quality
    D. graduation

17. When an employee training program fails, the most common reason is that

    A. training needs changed after the program had been implemented
    B. employees were not motivated
    C. there were no on-the-job rewards for behaviors and skills learned in training
    D. there were inaccurate training needs analyses

18. In implementing a progressive discipline pattern with a difficult employee, the first step is typically to

    A. issue a written warning to the employee
    B. impose a period of *decision leave* for the employee to consider his or her actions
    C. enroll the employee in additional training
    D. counsel or discuss the problem with the employee

19. The most widely used method of career planning that occurs in organizations is

    A. the planning workshop
    B. the extended seminar
    C. the self-assessment center
    D. counseling by supervisors and human resources staff

20. Under the provisions of the Equal Pay Act, differences in _____ is NOT a justification for paying a man more than a woman for the same job.

    A. performance
    B. skill
    C. family situations
    D. seniority

21. Compensation plans that protect the wages of workers hired before a certain date but start new workers at a lower pay rate are described as

    A. straight piecework
    B. weighted
    C. two-tiered
    D. differential piece rate

22. To prevent bias and legal complications, performance evaluations should steer clear of each of the following traits EXCEPT

    A. dependability
    B. knowledge
    C. attitude
    D. drive

23. The type of benefits most valued by employees are typically
    A. paid vacation and holidays
    B. medical
    C. long-term disability
    D. dental

24. Which of the following is the most common reason for employees to be opposed to the process of performance evaluation?
    A. Interference with normal work patterns
    B. Operating problems
    C. Bad system design
    D. Rater subjectivity

25. _____ training is most commonly used in the workplace.
    A. Apprenticeship
    B. Vestibule
    C. Cross-
    D. Classroom

KEY (CORRECT ANSWERS)

1.	D	11.	D
2.	A	12.	A
3.	B	13.	B
4.	B	14.	D
5.	B	15.	A
6.	B	16.	B
7.	C	17.	C
8.	D	18.	D
9.	B	19.	D
10.	C	20.	C

21. C
22. B
23. B
24. D
25. D

TEST 2

DIRECTIONS: Each question or incomplete statement is followed by several suggested answers or completions. Select the one that BEST answers the question or completes the statement. *PRINT THE LETTER OF THE CORRECT ANSWER IN THE SPACE AT THE RIGHT.*

1. In today's personnel market, the most critical factor used by recruiters to evaluate prospective job candidates who hold an MBA is usually the   1._____

    A. institution from which the degree was earned
    B. applicant's interpersonal style
    C. applicant's demonstrated skill level
    D. applicant's previous work experience

2. If a human resources manager decides to implement a preventive health care program in the workplace, he or she should be careful to guard against   2._____

    A. an increase in the number of medical claims made by employees
    B. a lack of quantifiable proof that the program is saving money or increasing productivity
    C. the splintering of the wellness program into its own budgetary status
    D. the abuse of available resources by employees

3. Competition is most likely to be a problem in performance evaluations that involve rating by   3._____

    A. the employee's subordinates
    B. the employee's peers
    C. self-evaluation
    D. a committee of several supervisors

4. Which of the following is not a problem commonly associated with merit pay systems?   4._____

    A. Employees often fail to make the connection between pay and performance.
    B. The size of merit awards has little effect on performance.
    C. Costs are usually higher than in individual incentive plans.
    D. The secrecy of rewards is seen as inequity by employees.

5. Which of the following step in the job analysis process is typically performed FIRST?   5._____

    A. Collecting data
    B. Selecting the jobs to be analyzed
    C. Determining how job analysis information will be used
    D. Preparing job descriptions

6. In which of the following sectors are employees typically most expensive to train?   6._____

    A. Consumer products
    B. Agriculture/forestry/fishing
    C. Services
    D. Industrial products

7. A commonly encountered disadvantage of using Bureau of Labor Statistics (BLS) data in pay surveys is that they

   A. tend to skew data in a way that favors labor over management
   B. are too generalized to be useful
   C. only list maximum and minimum pay rates, not medians and averages
   D. are not widely available to the public

8. Other than the salaries of training staff and trainees, which of the following is typically the largest expense involved in conducting an employee training program?

   A. Seminars and conferences
   B. Outside services
   C. Facilities and overhead
   D. Hardware

9. Under the provisions of the Equal Pay Act, differences in pay for equal work are permitted if they result from any of the following EXCEPT differences in

   A. seniority
   B. quality of performance
   C. age
   D. quantity or quality of production

10. Which of the following personnel selection procedures is typically LEAST costly?

    A. Background and reference checks
    B. Employment interview
    C. Preliminary screening
    D. Employment tests

11. Which of the following is a strictly internal method of personnel recruitment?

    A. Employment agencies
    B. Recruitment advertising
    C. Special-events recruiting
    D. Job posting

12. Of the following individual performance evaluation techniques, which has the advantage of offering the flexibility to discuss what the organization is attempting to accomplish?

    A. Graphic rating scale
    B. Behaviorally anchored rating scale (BARS)
    C. Essay evaluation
    D. Behavioral observation scale (BOS)

13. In human resources management, the *Pygmalion effect* refers to the tendency of an employee to

    A. live up to a manager's expectations
    B. identify with a working group
    C. sacrifice his or her personal life for improved work performance
    D. avoid work if at all possible

14. In medium-sized and larger organizations, the role of a human resources manager in the selection process is most often characterized by

    A. conducting the selection interview
    B. narrowing a field of applicants to a smaller, more manageable number
    C. designing the process by which candidates will be selected
    D. exercising final authority for hiring decisions

15. Employees who believe they have been discriminated against under the *whistleblowing* provisions of the Occupational Safety and Health Act may file a complaint at the nearest OSHA office within _____ of the alleged discriminatory action.

    A. 10 days   B. 30 days   C. 90 days   D. 6 months

16. Of the many applications possible with computerized human resource information systems, which of the following is most commonly used?

    A. Equal employment opportunity records
    B. Job analysis
    C. Performance appraisals
    D. Career pathing

17. _____ cost(s) is the term for expenditures for necessary items that do not become a part of a product or service.

    A. Operating supplies   B. Overhead
    C. Maintenance   D. Material

18. The union official who is responsible for representing the interests of local members in their relations with managers on the job is the

    A. president   B. business representative
    C. committee person   D. vice president

19. Of the many types of employment tests used in personnel selection, _____ tests tend to have the highest validities and reliabilities.

    A. performance simulation
    B. paper-and-pencil
    C. job sample performance
    D. personality and temperament

20. If an employee exhibits a *behavior discrepancy*—if his or her performance varies from what is expected on the job—a human resources manager might conduct a performance analysis. Most of these analyses begin with the process of

    A. motivating the employee to do better
    B. setting clear standards for performance on the job
    C. training the employee
    D. conducting a cost/value analysis of correcting the identified behavior

21. It is NOT a common goal of the orientation process to
    A. reduce personnel turnover
    B. reduce anxiety
    C. develop realistic expectations
    D. teach an employee specific job skills

22. In order for a situation to be accurately described as a job *layoff,* each of the following conditions must occur EXCEPT
    A. there is no work available
    B. the work shortage is sudden and surprising
    C. management expects the no-work situation to be temporary
    D. management intends to recall the employee

23. In a(n) _____ payroll plan, pay is based on two separate piecework rates: one for those who produce below or up to standard, and another for those who produce up to standard.
    A. equity
    B. Taylor
    C. functional
    D. distributive

24. Approximately what percentage of the U.S. labor force is currently unionized?
    A. 5   B. 15   C. 45   D. 70

25. The _____ principle states that managers should concentrate their efforts on matters that deviate from the normal and let their employees handle routine matters.
    A. critical-incident   B. flow-process   C. exception   D. democratic

KEY (CORRECT ANSWERS)

1. B		11. D	
2. B		12. C	
3. B		13. A	
4. C		14. B	
5. C		15. B	
6. D		16. A	
7. B		17. A	
8. C		18. C	
9. C		19. C	
10. C		20. D	

21. D
22. B
23. B
24. B
25. C

EXAMINATION SECTION
TEST 1

DIRECTIONS: Each question or incomplete statement is followed by several suggested answers or completions. Select the one that BEST answers the question or completes the statement. *PRINT THE LETTER OF THE CORRECT ANSWER IN THE SPACE AT THE RIGHT.*

1. Ms. Palmer is a manager who has the reputation of being tough, but fair-minded. She has just been promoted into a different part of the agency, and now heads a unit of thirty employees. She has observed that there are several employees who stick together. They seem to really enjoy working together, and she has observed them discussing how to solve work problems even on their lunch breaks. While she realizes they are effective and good at what they do, she does not like the idea of this informal work group staying together and possibly becoming more powerful and a threat to her authority. She decides to take steps to weaken its effectiveness.
The proposed action of Ms. Palmer is a

   A. *good* idea, since supervisors need complete control of their units
   B. *bad* idea, since the employees are having a good time and not causing trouble
   C. *good* idea, since the informal work group is most likely seen as a clique and resented by other employees
   D. *bad* idea, since the informal work group is functioning effectively, and she is most likely reacting in a defensive manner

1.____

2. The middle manager is both *player* and *coach* and needs to combine different skills and actions. A middle manager must see the *big picture,* be detached, and have a more long-range perspective. But he or she also needs to have detailed knowledge of the job, abundant job experience, and the ability to become deeply involved in the work.
It is sometimes difficult for a middle manager to know if he or she is employing the correct blend of these roles. Is he or she too involved in being a player—doing too many things that should be done by others? Or is he or she being too much of a coach—delegating too much and not being involved enough? How much one needs to be player or coach is unique to every situation and very much influenced, not only by the actual job to be done, but also by the needs and demands of bosses, co-workers, and employees.
With which of the following choices would the author MOST likely agree?

   A. When in doubt, a middle manager is likely to be better off delegating an assignment.
   B. If a middle manager has very competent employees, he or she is likely to be better off being a *player* than a *coach.*
   C. If a middle manager has a very demanding boss, he or she is likely to be better off being a *player.*
   D. If a situation calls for technical information that only the middle manager has, he or she is likely to be better off being a *player.*

2.____

3. Bob supervises fifteen employees in Unit 2, a position he has held for nine months. Before being promoted, he had worked in the same unit for four years and was well liked by all of his co-workers. He was an excellent employee and worked very hard. Bob has had a number of problems since receiving his promotion, however. A new employee in his unit seems to have an aversion to work. He frequently comes in late and makes many personal phone calls during the day. Bob has noticed this behavior, but is reluctant to do anything about it. Because he is not sure if the work he assigns the employee will get done, he gives much less work to him than to the others. Since the unit has a higher workload than ever, the work is piling up, and everyone in the unit is concerned.
One day, one of the personnel managers approaches Bob, tells him that the employees in the unit are upset about the situation, and urges him to take action. The next day, Bob calls a meeting of the staff and announces that *some people in the unit are coming in late, spending too much time on the phone, and not getting any work done.* He also says that this has to stop. That afternoon, Bob sends everyone in his unit a memo which emphasizes these points and bans any future personal calls in the office. Bob's way of handling this situation was

   A. *wise*, since this should have the effect of *shaping up* the other workers in the unit as well
   B. *unwise*, since it will lower productivity
   C. *unwise*, since it is too indirect and punitive a response
   D. *wise*, since he would have hurt the new employee's feelings if he had confronted him alone

4. You supervise a large unit of thirty employees. Diane, an employee in the unit, comes to you and says she can't work for Alan, her supervisor, anymore because he checks on her work all the time and is very critical of her.
She says she has tried to talk to him about the situation, but he won't listen to her.
Of the following, it would be BEST if you responded by saying

   A. "I'm sure Alan is treating you no differently than he treats everyone else"
   B. "Do you feel Alan is too critical of you?"
   C. "I don't think you should have gone over Alan's head by coming to me with this minor problem."
   D. "You wouldn't want Alan to accept poor quality work, would you?"

5. Which of the following statements is MOST accurate?

   A. It is much better for supervisors to focus on an employee's behavior rather than on his or her personality.
   B. It is not common for supervisors to procrastinate, hoping a problem will go away.
   C. Problems in working habits are always more difficult for supervisors to deal with than performance problems.
   D. When discussing an employee's behavior, it is wise for a supervisor to attribute motives to the behavior.

6. All of the following are likely to be true of a new supervisory situation EXCEPT:
    A. New supervisors are often on the spot during their first few weeks on the job
    B. Some new supervisors swell with responsibility instead of growing with it
    C. It is best if a new supervisor begins by making a lot of changes
    D. Former cronies of the new supervisor may expect special treatment and become resentful if it is not given

7. You have been the supervisor of a small unit for four months. One of the employees you supervise has consistently performed very poorly. You have talked with her on many occasions and evaluated her performance and set goals regularly. None of this has helped, although she does have the necessary skills to do the job. It seems that she just does not like to work very hard. She has been employed by the organization for thirty years, and other long-time employees have told you she has always performed poorly, but her other supervisors always overlooked her poor performance because they knew she would make a lot of trouble if she were formally disciplined. Your unit's workload has increased significantly in the past three months, and now the other employees must do a great deal of the work she is unwilling to do.
Of the following, which would be the BEST action for you to take?

    A. Discuss the situation with the employee and tell her you will have to begin formal discipline procedures if her performance does not improve.
    B. Ask the employee to resign.
    C. Ask one of the long-time employees to discuss the situation with her, encouraging her to resign.
    D. Ask your supervisor to fire her.

8. An employee you supervise is extremely competitive and very abrasive. The other employees in your unit are very resentful of this employee, who often *shows them up* with the very high quality of his work.
Of the following, it would be BEST if you

    A. let him know that, while you appreciate his concern and attempts to produce high quality work, the ability to get along with others and work as a team is just as important as technical ability
    B. ignore the situation, since his work is of such high quality
    C. let him know that, although you appreciate the high quality of his work, you can't help but get irritated by some of his behavior
    D. try to understand why he is acting the way he is

9. You have the responsibility of making a big decision, and you would like to get some group input.
Of the following, it is MOST important that you

    A. make sure everyone in the group has a chance to speak
    B. make it clear whether you will abide by their suggestions, or whether you just want to hear these suggestions to help you arrive at a possible solution
    C. wait until everyone has spoken before silently deciding whether to consider their ideas
    D. use good problem-solving techniques during the meeting

10. Which of the following statements is LEAST accurate?

    A. Most workers want to satisfy physical, social, and personal needs.
    B. A supervisor can have a significant impact upon an employee's personal life.
    C. Supervisors who emphasize getting to know the needs of their employees are not using their time wisely.
    D. Most workers want responsibilities they can handle, results they can demonstrate, and recognition for what they accomplish.

11. You are the supervisor of a unit of twenty employees. Janet, one of the employees, comes to you and says that Mark, her supervisor, is not supervising. She says he does not take the time to give her direction or feedback on her work. Janet also says that she often has had to do assignments that should have been handled by Mark. Janet understands that Mark has a large workload, but says that she does too. She has tried to talk to Mark several times about the situation, but says he won't acknowledge that there is a problem. Both Janet and Mark have performed well in the past.
    How would you handle this situation?

    A. Inform Janet that she should not have ignored the chain of command by going over Mark's head.
    B. Ask Janet to be more understanding of the pressures faced by Mark.
    C. Thank Janet for coming to you, but explain that there is nothing you can do.
    D. Discuss the situation with Mark.

12. It is now widely recognized that salaries, benefits, and working conditions have more of an impact on job satisfaction than on motivation. If they are not satisfactory, work performance and morale will suffer. But even when they are very good, employees will not necessarily be motivated to work well. For example, The Wall Street Journal recently reported that as many as 40% or 50% of newly hired Wall Street lawyers (whose salaries start at upwards of $90,000) quit within the first three years, citing long hours, pressures, and monotony as the prime offenders. It seems there is just not enough of an intellectual challenge in their jobs. An up-and-coming money-market executive concluded:
    Whether it was $1 million or $100 million, the procedure was the same. Except for the tension, a baboon could have done my job. When money and benefits are adequate, the most important additional determinants of job satisfaction are more responsibility, a sense of achievement, recognition, and a chance to advance. And all of these have a more significant influence on employee motivation and performance.
    If you were a supervisor who agreed with the above passage, which of the following would you MOST likely do?

    A. Press hard for large monetary bonuses for well-paid executives that you supervise
    B. Encourage employee involvement in establishing employee assistance programs
    C. Encourage employee participation in job design and decision-making
    D. Encourage *Employee of the Year* awards

13. A supervisor feels very comfortable with two of the employees she supervises because they have work styles very similar to her own.
    Of the following, the supervisor should

    A. feel confident that the employees are doing a very good job
    B. try to view their work as subjectively as possible
    C. try to view their work as objectively as possible
    D. carefully reevaluate their past work performance

14. Nelson is a perfectionist who often becomes overwhelmed because he is trying to do too much too well. He has extremely high expectations and seems to be showing signs of *burnout*. Nelson just cannot say no—he will take on anything, even if someone else could or should do it. And nothing leaves his desk unless it is done perfectly. You know he is taking a lot of work home with him in order to keep up.
    Assume that you are Nelson's supervisor.
    Which of the following do you feel would be the BEST way to handle the above situation?

    A. Enroll Nelson in a course on assertiveness.
    B. Discuss with Nelson the issues of working too hard and trying to be perfect and the consequences of these.
    C. Sit down with Nelson and let him know it is all right to make mistakes.
    D. Enroll Nelson in a course on establishing priorities.

15. Which of the following statements is LEAST accurate?

    A. In order to be highly productive, it usually does not matter whether a work group feels the general organizational climate is a fair and friendly one.
    B. Work groups are likely to contain an informal alignment based on status and authority.
    C. Supervisors should accept the subgroups that often form within work units.
    D. It is not desirable for a supervisor to be seen as an outsider imposing controls on members of the work group.

16. When conducting a corrective interview, a supervisor should do all of the following EXCEPT

    A. state the purpose of the interview
    B. change the employee's point of view
    C. state the problem, review expectations, and review the employee's current performance
    D. give time frames

17. Derogatory criticism of a person's work can be very harmful. A supervisor should be able to correct an employee without destroying his or her self-worth. A very minor example is a typist's mistake or typographical error that is sent back along with a 3x5 sheet of paper on which the typist's name is written, underlined, and deliberately misspelled. To me and the other typists in my department, it is a little degrading and implies a certain amount of ignorance and a lack of respect. Little things add up to a lot.
    Which of the following statements is BEST supported by the above passage?

A. Respect and dignity on the job are important to employees.
B. Supervisors should only criticize an employee's work when they absolutely have to.
C. A supervisor's ability to take criticism well is important in order to set an example for the supervisor's employees.
D. Give employees an inch and they'll take a mile.

18. You have just received a promotion to a different unit. Until he failed the oral exam for the title, Murray, a long-time and well-liked employee, had briefly held this position provisionally. You have been in the job for two weeks and have noticed that Murray is very bitter about the situation and is subtly undermining your authority. Of the following, it would be BEST if you

    A. had Murray transferred as soon as possible
    B. spoke with Murray about the situation
    C. spoke with your supervisor about the situation and asked him or her to talk with the employee
    D. ignored the situation for two more weeks to give Murray more time to adjust to it

19. *I believe that many of the problems I encountered were problems of fit with the informal organization. My peers and supervisors were unable to perceive me as being able to perform the job that the company hired me for. Their reaction to me was disbelief. I was out of the "place" normally filled by black people in the company; and since no black person had preceded me successfully, it was easy for my antagonists to believe I was inadequate, and to act as if I were.*
    – A black manager on his experience in the early 1960's
    Which of the following statements is BEST supported by the above passage?

    A. The informal organization is often beyond a supervisor's best efforts to control it.
    B. Expectations can significantly affect behavior and perceptions.
    C. Informal organizations wield little power.
    D. Informal organizations are very powerful.

20. You supervise a unit of twenty employees. Sometimes you must ask your employees to work overtime. You are careful to allocate the overtime fairly. Most of the employees are cooperative, but Andy always resists. Tonight he said that you deliberately pick him to work on Monday nights because you are afraid to ask anyone else to miss the football game on TV.
    Of the following, it would be BEST if you responded by saying:

    A. *"It's your own fault for always resisting overtime."*
    B. *"If you think you aren't getting a fair deal on over time, we can discuss it, but I do need you to work overtime tonight."*
    C. *"It's only a game. Besides, I've been fairly allocating overtime on Monday nights to every employee on a regular schedule."*
    D. *"I really don't think I've been singling you out."*

21. When supervising, it is BEST for supervisors to

    A. focus primarily on appearances
    B. refine their hidden expectations
    C. focus on an employee's attitude toward the job as a basis for performance evaluation
    D. know the job standards and be sure employees know them too

22. You are the manager of a large unit of fifty employees. Jane, a typist in the unit, comes to you with a complaint about her supervisor, Marie. Marie is a program analyst who transferred to your unit last year. Jane, a very good and reliable worker, tells you that Marie has been taking up a lot of the secretaries' and other workers' time by talking with them a great deal about projects she is working on. Jane says she realizes that Marie is insecure about her work and needs a lot of support, but her behavior is causing some disruption. Because you are Marie's supervisor, she asks you to intervene.
Of the following choices, it would be BEST if you

    A. went over Marie's personnel records for clues of poor performance and then discuss the situation with her
    B. told Jane she should have gone directly to Marie to discuss the problem, instead of coming to you
    C. asked Jane for more proof
    D. called Marie in to ask her how she is doing, and asked if you could do anything to make her feel more comfortable on the job

23. Of the following statements, which would MOST likely be appropriate for a supervisor to say to someone he or she supervises?

    A. "I'm concerned about the impact your long coffee breaks are having on the other employees. I'd like you to shorten them."
    B. "Time off next week? You must be kidding!"
    C. "You must be pretty thirsty to take all those long coffee breaks."
    D. "I get annoyed every time I see you coming in late."

24. When Napoleon was asked why he reinstituted the symbolic and practically worthless Legion of Honor Medal, he replied, *you lead men by baubles, not words.*
Another way to say that would be that a supervisor

    A. gives all of the employees she supervises *outstanding* evaluations
    B. never overly praises those he supervises
    C. passes out trophies annually to outstanding employees
    D. praises those she supervises only when they deserve it

25. All of the following are common problems faced by new supervisors EXCEPT

    A. difficulty in making decisions because of the fear of making a mistake
    B. spending too much time procrastinating or collecting data before making a decision
    C. success in delegating work
    D. succumbing to waves of inertia because of fear

KEY (CORRECT ANSWERS)

1.	D	11.	D
2.	D	12.	C
3.	C	13.	C
4.	B	14.	B
5.	A	15.	A
6.	C	16.	B
7.	A	17.	A
8.	A	18.	B
9.	B	19.	B
10.	C	20.	B

21. D
22. A
23. A
24. C
25. C

———

TEST 2

DIRECTIONS: Each question or incomplete statement is followed by several suggested answers or completions. Select the one that BEST answers the question or completes the statement. *PRINT THE LETTER OF THE CORRECT ANSWER IN THE SPACE AT THE RIGHT.*

1. Which of the following is NOT true about planning and organizing work? 1.____

   A. Good planning skills are not as important as good people skills.
   B. Well-written operating manuals and other guides can allow a supervisor to primarily manage by exception.
   C. Every operation needs planning, even when it looks routine.
   D. A good supervisor should have alternatives readily available for potential problems that are predictable.

2. Two weeks ago, you asked one of your employees to be sure to keep a copy of all mail-in requests that come in to your office requesting information about an important project. You have just found out he has not been doing it. He explains that he thought you said it would be *nice* if he kept copies. You are quite upset about this. Of the following, it would be BEST if you 2.____

   A. tried to find out how the possible misunderstanding occurred and ask him to follow your instructions
   B. tried to find out how the possible misunderstanding occurred and then ask him if he is willing to keep the copies
   C. assigned the task to someone else
   D. told him that when you say *it would be nice if,* you mean he should do something

3. You have just been appointed supervisor of a large unit of thirty employees. You immediately notice there is a sort of *caste system* in the office, which runs along salary-grade lines. Although it is in their job descriptions, certain employees are not allowed to answer the phone when it rings. They must wait for a higher-grade employee to answer it. The slightly higher-grade employees have a number of privileges and also get to decide things like when the blinds should be open. There is a great deal of divisiveness in the unit.
Of the following, it would be BEST if you 3.____

   A. waited at least a month before taking any sort of action in order to acquire more information
   B. held a staff meeting as soon as possible to discuss the situation
   C. asked the former supervisor why things had gotten to this stage
   D. slowly, but firmly, began changing policies

4. Seymour seems allergic to detail. He thinks of himself as a man of action who gets right to the heart of the issue–and very often he does. He hands in his work early, but occasionally it needs to be redone because a key detail has been overlooked. Seymour is a very valuable, intelligent employee, who has a lot of enthusiasm. You have noticed, however, that this enthusiasm for undertaking new projects sometimes gets in the way of his follow-through.
If you were Seymour's supervisor, which of the following do you feel would be the BEST way to handle the above situation? 4.____

A. Whenever possible, assign a co-worker who is good at handling details to work on projects with Seymour.
B. Discuss the matter honestly with Seymour and order him to change his work habits.
C. Anonymously send Seymour an article on the importance of attention to detail and of follow-through.
D. Discuss the matter honestly with Seymour and ask him to establish work goals.

5. You supervise a small unit of five employees. The day before you are about to leave for a much needed and well-deserved two-week vacation abroad, the most competent worker asks to speak privately with you. The employee tells you that she has just been offered a better paying job with another organization. She is the employee who has been in the unit the longest and knows a great deal of valuable information about procedures and tasks that the other employees do not know. There has been talk for a while of upgrading her position.
Of the following, it would be BEST if you

   A. sincerely stated that you do not want to stand in her way, congratulate her, and let her know that you will miss her very much
   B. changed procedures so that never again would so much expertise be left to just one employee
   C. discussed the matter fully with the employee, and if she wished to stay with your unit, assured her that you would instruct your replacement supervisor to immediately begin the process of upgrading her
   D. discussed the matter with the employee, letting her know how valuable she is, and then asked her to stay long enough to train someone fully before she leaves

6. You have assigned a new project to one of the employees you supervise. Soon after the assignment, she comes into your office and asks that you give the project to another worker. She feels she is not qualified to complete it correctly and that she will do a poor job.
Of the following, it would be BEST if you

   A. urged her to complete the project because this is a golden opportunity for her to shine
   B. allowed her to express her doubts, and then provided support in helping her organize and master the project
   C. reassigned the project to someone who would like to do it
   D. asked her why she is so insecure about doing the project

7. All of the following are true EXCEPT:
   A. Support on the job can reduce stress
   B. An employee's self-esteem is rarely a critical determinant of performance
   C. Employees who are allowed to participate in making decisions about how a task is to be performed are more enthusiastic about the task and are more likely to do the task well
   D. A supervisor's behavior has a greater effect on his or her employees than most supervisors recognize

8. *Our control systems are designed under the apparent assumption that ninety percent of the people are lazy ne'er-do-wells, just waiting to lie, cheat, steal.... We demoralize the ninety-five percent of the workforce who do act like adults by designing systems to cover our tails against the five percent who are bad actors.*
   A supervisor who believed the above statement would MOST likely

   A. give employees more discretion in performing tasks
   B. supervise employees very closely
   C. supervise problem employees more loosely than other supervisors would
   D. give employees less discretion in performing tasks

9. All of the following are common problems found in new supervisors EXCEPT

   A. an over- or underestimation of what they can accomplish
   B. an unwillingness to accept positive feedback from those they supervise
   C. overly flattering behavior towards their supervisors
   D. a tendency to become overly concerned with appearance rather than substance

10. Phyllis is a typist who works in a small typing pool. She has worked there for a year and a half, and has received excellent evaluations. Phyllis is a 24-year-old white female. Her supervisor is Patricia, a 45-year-old white female. They have always gotten along well, and morale in the unit is good. There are five white females and one Hispanic female in the unit.
    One night, Phyllis and her husband, who is black, ran into Patricia and her husband as they were leaving the movie theater. Phyllis noticed that Patricia seemed uncomfortable, but didn't think much more about it. The following Monday, Patricia asked Phyllis how she enjoyed the movie. She also asked if that was Phyllis' husband with her. When Phyllis replied that it was, Patricia gave her a weak smile, talked a little more, and left. Since that time, Patricia has been quite cold to Phyllis. For the last month, Phyllis has noticed that she has been getting all of the assignments for typing tabular material and other difficult typing that no one else wants. Previously, this work had been evenly distributed among all of the typists.
    The above passage is an example of

    A. comparable worth
    B. subtle discrimination
    C. sexual harassment
    D. equal pay for equal work

11. At a staff meeting, another supervisor made a comment that you felt was very critical of your department. You are about to meet with him in his office.
    Of the following, it would be BEST if you said,

    A. "I really didn't appreciate that comment you made about my department during the staff meeting."
    B. "That sure was an interesting staff meeting. I learned a lot. How about you?"
    C. "I was concerned about your comments on my department this morning. Do you have any suggestions on how I might improve things?"
    D. "I was interested in what you had to say today in the staff meeting. I feel some of your remarks were critical of my department, and I'd like to talk with you about them."

12. Donna's style has no doubt increased her supervisor's risk of heart attack significantly. She is a procrastinator and a last minute operator. She seems to thrive on the challenge of these self-imposed tight deadlines. Her supervisor has even tried lying and pushing the deadline of a project up a week before it was really due, but somehow she always finds out the truth. The quality of her work is excellent, but her supervisor never can be sure a project will be finished on time. Her supervisor feels he could not constantly work under that sort of stress and cannot imagine that Donna is not going to succumb to the pressure one of these days and miss a deadline. Besides, he feels all that stress is not good for her health.
The BEST way to handle the above situation is for Donna's superior to

    A. do nothing
    B. call her in to his office and lecture her about the importance of not procrastinating
    C. anonymously send her a book on planning and time management
    D. threaten her with severe formal disciplinary action unless she stops procrastinating

13. Barbara is an employee who has a reputation for being a troublemaker. She comes to her supervisor, Jack Burns, and says she is being sexually harassed. Barbara accuses Jack's superior, David London, who has been a close friend of Jack's for many years.
Jack should

    A. take Barbara's complaint seriously
    B. refer Barbara to counseling or to an employee assistance program
    C. listen to Barbara sympathetically, advise her to go to the affirmative action office to file a complaint, but also warn David that a complaint is going to be filed against him
    D. ask Barbara if she has any documentation to support her allegations

14. Which of the following statements about supervision is LEAST accurate?

    A. Once an employee performs well, he or she will continue to perform at that level.
    B. It is important for supervisors to encourage the employees they supervise to employ good delegation skills.
    C. Hidden expectations a supervisor may have, like assuming an employee does not mind taking work home, can be harmful.
    D. Supervisors should always be trying to improve their supervisory skills.

15. Which of the following would NOT be considered an example of subtle discrimination against an employee who is a protected class member?
A superior

    A. protects a protected class member by never giving negative feedback and by giving easy assignments
    B. asks a highly respected protected class member in the unit to talk with a Hispanic employee about a performance problem
    C. treats black male employees with more respect than she treats white male employees
    D. shares important information much more with male employees than with female employees

16. You supervise eight employees. In order to protect all of them from eyestrain, one particular assignment that requires close eyework is rotated and shared by everyone. One of the employees has just complained to you that he receives more of this work than the others, and he wants to be excused from doing the work today. You are not completely sure that he is incorrect.
Of the following, it would be BEST if you responded by saying:

    A. "*Let me review my records to see if I have assigned the work fairly, and I will get right back to you.*"
    B. "*I have given a lot of thought to how assignments are allocated, and it is fair for everyone. Please go back to work.*"
    C. "*Last week you complained about needing a new electric stapler. The week before, you said you lost money in the vending machine. Isn't there anything you like around here?*"
    D. "*I am really sorry things have worked out this way, but I have to ask you to do the work anyway.*"

16.____

17. Morgan works very, very hard but is not as productive as he could be, considering how hard he works. He seems to have a hard time setting priorities and determining what is really important. There have been a number of occasions when you have found him hard at work on projects that were of much lower priority than others that were sitting on his desk. He also loves to collect information and thinks tons of information (some relevant, some not) will help him make the *perfect decision.*
If you were Morgan's supervisor, which of the following do you feel would be the BEST way to handle the above situation?

    A. Sit down with him and assist him in improving his decision–making skills.
    B. Meet with him to discuss your observations and then review his projects, establish priorities, and set realistic goals together
    C. Have him attend a training course on improving self–esteem
    D. Have him attend a training program on improving decision–making skills

17.____

18. *A few years back, I had the occasion to work at an agency where a new manager came in. We soon found out that the happy atmosphere we had all enjoyed for the past few years was slowly eroding. We started receiving memos for everything and anything; such as no more placing sweaters on chairs, absolutely clear desk tops, personal chattering is forbidden at all times, compulsory signing in and out at lunch time, and so on. This soon brought a big change in our health. We got nervous stomachs, headaches, high blood pressure, and so on. He also stated that women were taking men's jobs away and should be at home. Many of us spoke to the higher-ups, but nothing was done. So now I had to make a big decision. I loved my job but not the atmosphere I was working in. I was fortunate in having a friend who helped me to get into another agency where I still work. This atmosphere caused quite a few more people to leave, and it was a big shame because we all were good, productive workers. In fact, in many cases the agency had to hire two workers to do the job one of us had been able to do so well.*
What could the administrators have done to avoid the above situation?

18.____

A. Conducted exit interviews of the employees who left to determine their reasons for leaving
B. Instituted the above changes more slowly
C. Realized the changes were hurting employee morale and withdrawn them
D. Used the carrot-and-stick approach to management

19. John is a 25-year-old black training specialist trainee in Agency X. He has been with the agency for eight months. John works with Ed, a 28-year-old white training specialist who has been in his position for four years. Their supervisor is Daniel, a 30-year-old white male who has been supervisor for six years. Daniel and Ed are good friends. John has become upset because he and Ed are treated so differently. Ed is allowed to come in late and leave early. On days when Ed drives his car to the office, he is allowed to leave every 90 minutes to change his parking place so that he won't get a parking ticket. Ed never has to let Daniel know where he is going or what meetings he is attending. John is not allowed any leave violations, however minor. The second time he was a few minutes late to work, Daniel called him in to his office and reprimanded him. There is a training conference in Washington, D.C. that Ed and Daniel are going to. John has asked permission to go, but has been told he cannot go because he would not benefit as much as Ed and Daniel would.
Of the following statements, which BEST applies to the above paragraph?

19.____

A. Bad supervision can look a lot like discrimination.
B. Friends should never work together.
C. Agencies should provide parking for their employees in order to improve productivity and reduce friction.
D. Supervisors should be careful in choosing when to reprimand employees.

20. All of the following are common problems faced by new supervisors EXCEPT:

20.____

A. One's former peers are now people one has to supervise, and this can lead to confusion, conflict, or resentment
B. The supervisor may have been *top dog* in the previous title and now has to start at the *bottom* in the new position; this can lead to arrogant or defensive behavior
C. New supervisors usually experience low levels of stress
D. The new supervisor is often selected because he or she was a very competent employee, not because he or she demonstrated leadership or supervisory skills, and the lack of these skills can lead to serious problems with those he or she supervises

KEY (CORRECT ANSWERS)

1. A
2. A
3. D
4. A
5. C

6. B
7. B
8. A
9. B
10. B

11. D
12. A
13. A
14. A
15. C

16. A
17. B
18. C
19. A
20. C

www.ingramcontent.com/pod-product-compliance
Lightning Source LLC
Chambersburg PA
CBHW082212300426
44117CB00016B/2782